THE
PRONUNCIATION OF SPANISH

THE PRONUNCIATION

OF

SPANISH

BY

WILLIAM F. STIRLING, B.A.

CAMBRIDGE
AT THE UNIVERSITY PRESS
1935

CAMBRIDGE
UNIVERSITY PRESS

University Printing House, Cambridge CB2 8BS, United Kingdom

Cambridge University Press is part of the University of Cambridge.

It furthers the University's mission by disseminating knowledge in the pursuit of education, learning and research at the highest international levels of excellence.

www.cambridge.org
Information on this title: www.cambridge.org/9781316509722

© Cambridge University Press 1935

First published 1935
First paperback edition 2015

A catalogue record for this publication is available from the British Library

ISBN 978-1-316-50972-2 Paperback

CONTENTS

PREFACE

THIS book is intended to fill a gap in Spanish studies. So far as I know, there is no book which deals with Spanish pronunciation, in a manner which is particularly adapted for the use of English people. Indeed, it is the need for a book of this kind which has led me to collect my notes, taken in conversation with educated Spaniards. These I hope will be of assistance to English people who travel in Spain; but the principal object of the book is to enable English students of the Spanish language to acquire a good Spanish pronunciation, particularly if they contemplate teaching it.

In Spain, four languages are spoken—Galician, Basque, Spanish and Catalan. Spanish is divided into two main dialects—Castilian and Andalusian. Andalusian differs from Castilian chiefly in pronunciation. The mother-language, which originated in the north-east of Castile, is Castilian or Spanish. The Spanish pronunciation dealt with in this book is educated Castilian, such as is spoken in Madrid to-day.

For representing speech-sounds, two systems of notation, or rather, two varieties of the same system, are employed: an approximate or "broad" transcription, obtained by using the minimum number of phonetic symbols without causing ambiguity, and a more minute or "narrow" transcription, which aims at expressing the sounds of spoken Spanish with the greatest possible exactitude. Generally speaking, I have used the system of phonetic notation adopted by the International Phonetic Association, but I have ventured to introduce a few innovations, in cases where it seems to me the learner will be helped thereby. For instance, members of the same phoneme, that is sounds which do not change the meaning of a word when substituted for each other, like b and ƀ, require only one symbol in a broad transcription (b), since the difference in their pronunciation is due solely to their position in a word or word-group. In my view, this gives insufficient guidance to the learner, particularly when he sees words like *basta* and *haba*, where b is plosive in the first case but fricative in the second, transcribed with the same symbol for b. In the opinion of many teachers, rules are not enough; the difference must be expressed visually. For this reason, many sounds which are members of the same phoneme are transcribed with different symbols throughout this book, although the transcription is broad in other respects. Whether one symbol shall be used to represent all the sounds comprised in a phoneme is a matter for the individual teacher to decide; some manage better without differentiating the two members of the b phoneme, while others find such differentiation a help for distinguishing the two sounds they represent.

There are two features of Spanish pronunciation which should be mastered by the English learner as soon as possible. Without them, he will always appear to Spanish people to be speaking with a strong "foreign accent". These two features are (1) the peculiar Spanish "intonation", the rise and fall of the voice, and (2) the characteristic Spanish omission of the "glottal stop", that slight consonantal sound before words which begin with a vowel, which, if used in Spanish, prevents the syllables of a group of words or "word-group" from running fluently together. Intonation is a subject which many consider to have been inadequately treated in the past, even by phoneticians; it needs a book to itself, illustrated by examples in musical notation. But since it is essential for a foreigner learning

Spanish to have some idea of what intonation implies, the out-lines of Spanish intonation, based on personal observations, have been included in a chapter at the end of the present volume. There, intonation has been shown by a system of dots, stressed syllables being marked by bigger dots than unstressed syllables.

As to the glottal stop and the means for avoiding it (for most English people, when they begin to speak Spanish, use the glottal stop at every opportunity, although they are quite un-aware of the fact), I have used a linking-mark to signify that final consonants must be joined to initial vowels. This should help beginners, by reminding them visually, that the words are not spoken separately but are run together. Thus the two words

Un hombre

are run together so as to sound like unombre, transcribed in this book as

u'n‿ombre.

A bracket like this is generally used to show the occurrence of "synaloepha" (see § 69 (b)) or elision. Its use, in each of these three ways, impresses on the learner's mind the fact that two vowels joined by a bracket form part of one syllable only. Thus eso es is transcribed e'so‿es, two syllables (the stroke before s, and before n in the preceding example, shows that the following syllable is stressed).

The following list of books will be of interest to students of Spanish pronunciation and of phonetics in general:

1. Navarro Tomás, T. *Manual de Pronunciación Española.*
   Madrid: Revista de Filología española, 1932. 4th ed.
2. Menéndez Pidal, R. *Manual de Gramática Histórica.*
   Madrid: Suárez, 1929. 5th ed., 2nd imp.

3. Colton, M. A. *La Phonétique Castillane.* Paris: Imprimerie Lievens à Saint-Maur (Seine), 1909.
4. *Revista de Filología Española* (published monthly). Madrid: Centro de Estudios Históricos.
5. Passy, P. *Petite Phonétique Comparée.* Leipzig: Teubner.
6. Jones, D. *Outline of English Phonetics.* Leipzig: Teubner, 1934.
7. Publications of the International Phonetic Association, obtainable from the Secretary, Professor Daniel Jones, University College, London.

I am under personal obligation to Professor Daniel Jones, both for permission to use Diagram No. 1, from his *Outline of English Phonetics,* and for the invaluable assistance which he has so generously given me in preparing this book for the press. I am also indebted to Miss Lilias Armstrong, who has given me permission to use several diagrams which I have adapted from those in her book *The Phonetics of French* (Bell, 1932).

WILLIAM F. STIRLING

UNIVERSITY COLLEGE
LONDON

July 1935

TABLE OF SPANISH SPEECH-SOUNDS

Consonants	Bi-labial	Labio-dental	Dental	Alveolar	Palatal	Velar
Plosive	p b		t d	c (ɟ)		k g
Nasal	m	(ɱ)		n	ɲ	(ŋ)
Lateral				l (ɫ)	ʎ	
Rolled				rr		
Flapped				r		
Fricative	(ƀ)	f	θ (θ̬) (đ)	s (ş)	[ç]	x (ǥ)
Semi-vowel	w				j	{w}

Vowels					Front	Back
Close					i	u
Half-close					e	o
Half-open					(ɛ)	
Open					a	(ɑ) (ɔ)

( ) indicate subsidiary members of phonemes.

[ ] indicate an alternative sound.

} indicate a secondary articulation.

CHAPTER I

ON THE USE OF PHONETIC SYMBOLS

1. The following is a complete list of symbols used in a narrow transcription of Spanish:

Symbol	Example	Symbol	Example
(a) VOWELS			
i	ví	ɑ	bajo
e	canté	ɔ	corredor
ɛ	perro	o	polo
a	cata	u	tú
(b) DIPHTHONGS			
eọ	beodo	ɑọ	caoba
eụ	deuda	ɑụ	incauto
ɛị	peine	ɔị	hoy
aị	hay	oụ	bou
(c) CONSONANTS			
p	popa	ɲ	año
b	bomba	ŋ	cinco
t	tinto	l	hilo
d	donde	ł	vulgo
c	hacha	ʎ	olla
ɉ	ya	rr	parra
k	cuenco	r	para
g	ganga	ƀ	haba
m	amo	f	café
ɱ	infante	θ	hizo
n	uno	θ̬	juzgar

Symbol	Example	Symbol	Example
đ	miđo	x	oj̇o
s	oso	g̣	peg̣ar
ş	mismo	w	huésped
ç	¡ay!	j	haya

o placed above or below the symbol for a voiced consonant, indicates that it is voiceless.

v placed above or below the symbol for a voiceless consonant, indicates that it is voiced.

ǁ indicates emphatic stress on the following syllable.

ǀ indicates normal stress on the following syllable.

ː is placed after a sound to indicate that it is long.

~ is placed over a vowel to indicate that it is nasalised.

2. It is important that phonetic symbols should be used correctly, and not abused. No symbol must be taught until the pupil has learned to recognise the sound it represents; in this way, each new symbol will have its own sound, and not be confused with the orthography. Symbols should be constantly used, once they have been learned.

3. EAR-TRAINING. As soon as the pupil has been taught two or three speech-sounds, the teacher should repeat them aloud, varying the order, for dictation. If the pupil cannot distinguish one sound from another, they should be repeated to him very slowly until he notices the difference. When all the sounds in Spanish have been studied, there will be an almost endless variety of combinations of sounds (which have, of course, no meaning) for dictation. These "meaningless words" may, at a later stage, be even further complicated by the addition of sounds from other languages. It is a good plan for the teacher to read out a short passage in Spanish, from time to time, to be taken down in phonetic symbols. This will

ensure that the pupil is transcribing what he *hears*, and not what he thinks he *ought to hear*.

4. PHONETIC TRANSCRIPTIONS. At least once a week the pupil should transcribe, as far as he is able, a passage of Spanish, and all the mistakes should be carefully noted. Phonetic transcriptions should be read aloud in oral classes.

5. All the examples should be repeated aloud to make sure that they are properly understood. It cannot be urged sufficiently that practice is essential in learning the pronunciation of a language, and if a pupil is supervised by a native or a qualified teacher, he should soon make good progress. No book can teach a sound, but it can give indications of how to make a sound, and thus lay a groundwork of knowledge on which to base a fluent pronunciation, which comes only with constant practice and association with fluent speakers.

CHAPTER II

ON THE MAKING OF SPEECH-SOUNDS

6. When we speak, the breath passes slowly from the larynx and goes out through the mouth or the nasal cavity, or both. The resultant sound is dependent upon two things: the position of the vocal cords, and the position or movement of the organs of articulation.

7. THE VOCAL CORDS. The vocal cords are two membranes in the larynx which can be vibrated. The space between the cords, called the *glottis*, can be closed and opened again, causing a plosion or plosive consonant, written ? in phonetic notation.

This sound, which is used in English, most Germanic languages and Arabic, is not heard in Spanish.

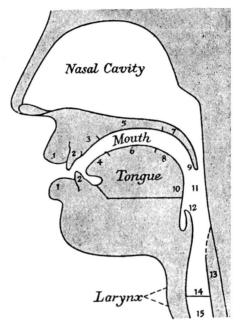

Diagram No. 1. Organs of Articulation

1, lips; 2, teeth; 3, alveolar or teeth ridge; 4, blade of tongue; 5, hard palate; 6, front of tongue; 7, soft palate or velum; 8, back of tongue; 9, uvula; 10, root of tongue; 11, pharyngal cavity (pharynx); 12, epiglottis; 13, oesophagus or food passage; 14, position of vocal cords; 15, wind-pipe

8. When the vocal cords are loosely closed, a passage of air causes them to vibrate: this vibration is called *voice*. No voice is heard when the vocal cords are wide apart. When voice is

added to a sound made by the air in its passage through the mouth or the nasal cavity, the process is called *voicing*. Voicing is given to *voiceless* consonants to make them *voiced*.

Examples: **p, t, k** (voiceless) and **b, d, g** (voiced).

9. The vocal cords may also be partially closed, and the resulting sound, when air is breathed through the glottis, is a whisper.

10. ORGANS OF ARTICULATION. Diagram No. 1 shows that there are many organs which are used in the articulation of speech-sounds. Some of these organs of articulation are movable.

11. THE LIPS. The lips may be pressed together as for **p, b, m**, or the lower lip may touch the upper teeth as in **f, v.** They may be rounded as for **o** and **u**, or they may be spread as for **i**.

12. THE TONGUE. The blade, which includes the tip, the front and the back of the tongue are all movable. By moving the tip we make **t, d, n, l, r**, etc. By changing the position of the front of the tongue we can move from **i** to **a**, and by raising the back, we can change from **a** to **u**.

13. THE SOFT PALATE. This is used as a trap-door between the pharynx and the nasal cavity. When the soft palate is lowered, the resulting speech-sound is given a nasal quality and is called *nasal*, since the whole or part of the air-stream passes through the nasal cavity. When the soft palate is raised, no air can pass through the nasal cavity.

Examples: Compare **b, d** (soft palate raised) and **m, n** (soft palate lowered).

14. THE UVULA. The movement of the uvula has no part in the pronunciation of Spanish or English, but examples of its use may be heard in the Parisian *r*'s (a rolled uvular *r*,

ʀ, and a fricative uvular *r*, ʁ) and in the Arabic voiceless plosive, q.

15. The movable organs can, of course, be put in many other positions, and are so used for other languages.

16. If we raise the soft palate and allow a voiced sound to pass through the mouth, without audibly impeding its progress,

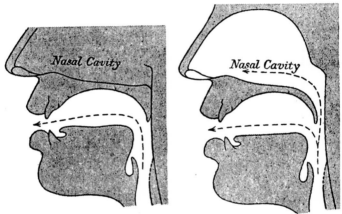

Diagram No. 2. Movement of the Soft Palate

we are articulating a *vowel*, or more particularly, an *oral vowel*. A *nasal vowel* is made when the same conditions are observed, save for a lowering of the soft palate (see Diagram No. 2).

17. Any speech-sound which is not a vowel is called a *consonant*.

18. VOWELS. Vowels are classified according to the position of the tongue. If the front of the tongue is raised as high as possible, without causing friction, we can make a sound which marks the limit of vowel production. This is called a *cardinal* vowel, and is represented by the symbol i. If we lower and

retract the tongue, as far as possible without causing friction, we mark the opposite limit of vowel production; this is cardinal vowel a. Intermediate vowels (e, ε and a) are chosen so as to give four equal degrees of acoustic separation between i and a. ɔ, o and u continue the same series of equal degrees of acoustic separation along the line of back vowels.

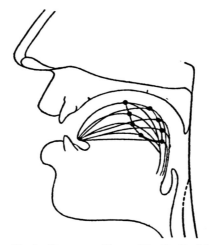

Diagram No. 3. Tongue positions of the Cardinal Vowels

19. There is no cardinal vowel in English or Spanish, but three, i, ε and a, are used in French. The same symbols are used in English and Spanish, to represent those vowels which are nearest the cardinal vowels.

20. The position of any vowel could be shown on Diagram No. 3, but for practical purposes a straight-line figure, joining i, a, a and u, is used.

21. When the front of the tongue is raised, the vowel is said

to be a *close front vowel*, and when it is lowered, the vowel is called an *open front vowel*. Similarly, by raising and lowering the back of the tongue, we have a *close back vowel* and an *open back vowel*. Vowels which are neither close nor open are classified as *half-close* or *half-open* (see Diagram No. 4).

22. DIPHTHONGS. A *diphthong* is a gliding sound, in which the organs of speech start in the position of one vowel-sound, and immediately proceed in the direction of another. Whether a word contains a pure vowel or a diphthong is a matter to be determined aurally, and the fact that a letter is formed of two ligatured vowel-letters, such as æ, œ, does not mean that its sound is a diphthong. This is a popular error due to confusion with digraph.

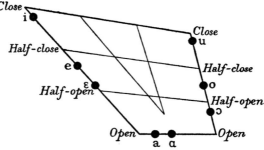

Diagram No. 4. The Spanish Vowels

CHAPTER III

FRONT VOWELS

23. There are three front vowels in Spanish, **i**, **e** and **a**. None of these sounds occurs in educated southern English and the learner must not confuse them with similar English sounds, some of which are diphthongs.

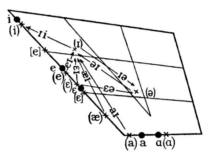

Diagram No. 5. The Spanish Front Vowels and the vowel-sounds substituted for them by English learners
( ) denote English vowels   [ ] denote French vowels

i

24. EXAMPLES: *y* i, *dí* di, *ribera* rri'ɓera, *hijo* 'ixo, *Madrid* ma'ðri, *villa* 'biʎa, *mirra* 'mirra, *sitio* 'sitjo, *ahí* a'i.

25. DESCRIPTION: The front of the tongue is raised to a very close position, and the lips are spread. The space between the teeth is the same as for the English vowel-sound in *see*. The soft palate is raised. Greater energy must be used than in English.

26. ARTICULATION: To make i, the tip of the tongue must

be pressed against the lower teeth; the pupil must then spread
his lips and say the English vowel i (as in *sea*) with great
energy. If he speaks educated southern English, the result
should be a perfect Spanish i. Sometimes the tongue position
is too high and friction is heard. In this case it is quite simple
to avoid causing friction and therefore to lower the tongue to
the required position. Unfortunately, English people do not all
have the same pronunciation: while some pronounce *sea*, siː,
others say sɪi or səɪ (ɪ is the vowel-sound in *bit* and ə is the final
vowel-sound in *mother*). In teaching i, the following method
should be tried if the pupil does not use a pure vowel in his
pronunciation of *sea*. By watching his mouth in a mirror he
can see how his tongue moves slightly while he says the word
sea. For the Spanish word *si*, his tongue must not move at all,
and his tongue must remain in the same position the whole
time. Once the diphthong element has been removed, the
vowel may be taught in the normal way.

27. *-ir*: the ending *-ir* (ir) is usually mispronounced ɪə by
English learners. i and r should first be practised separately,
the pause between them always growing smaller until they can
be said together.

28. Unstressed i must be as well pronounced as stressed i.
Example: *imitar* is pronounced imiˈtar, not ɪmɪˈtaː.

29. EXERCISES:

(a) Practise i long, then short. Alternate with English i and ɪ.

(b) Read out several times:

    pi, bi, ti, di, etc.
    ip, ib, it, id, etc.
    iris ˈiris, *insistir* insisˈtir, *inhibir* iniˈbir, *crisis* ˈkrisis,
    vigil biˈxil, *tris* tris, *sillín* siˈʎin, *Cid* θið, *quintín* kinˈtin.

(c) Contrast, reading aloud:

English		Spanish	
ear	ɪə	*ir*	ir
a key	ə ˈkiː	*aquí*	aˈki
see	siː	*sí*	si
meeting	ˈmitɪŋ	*mitin*	ˈmitin
militia	mɪˈlɪʃə	*milicia*	miˈliθja

e

30. EXAMPLES: *pero* ˈpero, *reo* ˈrreo, *lejos* ˈlexos, *parezca* paˈreθka, *desdicha* desˈdicha, *sierpe* ˈsjerpe, *mes* mes, *piel* pjel, *haber* aˈƀer, *pecho* ˈpeco.

31. DESCRIPTION: The front of the tongue is raised to a position about half-way between the positions for an open and for a close front vowel. The soft palate is raised.

32. ARTICULATION: As the diagram shows, e is between French e (as in *et*) and French ɛ (as in *est*). It should therefore be easy for students of French to learn the Spanish vowel. The vowel-sound which the English learner usually substitutes for e is the diphthong eɪ, as in southern English *day*: in other dialects of English, ɛɪ, æɪ, and even aɪ are used. Scots sometimes pronounce *day* with a pure e. A good way of learning e is to try and isolate the first part of eɪ; this sometimes gives too open a sound, in which case the vowel should be slightly modified in the direction of i, thus raising the tongue to the required degree of closeness. Another plan is to begin with the English ɛ, as in *bed*, and to aim at a sound between this and i. If both these methods fail, take the English vowel ɪ, lengthen it and make it more like ɛ. The result should be a fairly good e. For those who normally use ɛɪ, æɪ or aɪ for eɪ in English, one of the last two methods should be used. For

the more open variety of e, which is used in certain cases (see below), the student should make his e more like the English ɛ. The open e is much easier to learn than the close e. The only difficulty occurs in the ending -er, where English pupils will use the diphthong ɛə (as in *there*). This can be avoided in the same way as ɪə instead of ir. Take the open e and r separately, and then gradually join them.

33. **Unstressed e.** This must be well articulated: *descender* desθenˈder, *corredor* korreˈdor.

34. **Open e.** e is variable, and depends on its surroundings for its pronunciation. The difference in pronunciation is not normally marked in phonetic transcriptions, but for narrow transcriptions open e is represented by the symbol ɛ: this will be used, for the sake of clearness, in the examples illustrating the following rules on the use of e and ɛ:

35. (1) e is used in all open syllables,[1] unless it is preceded or followed by rr, or is followed by x, when ɛ must be used.

Examples:

pero ˈpero, *canté* kanˈte, *pecho* ˈpeco, *señal* seˈɲal;

but *remo* ˈrrɛmo, *corregidor* korrɛxiˈdor, *perro* ˈpɛrro, *quejas* ˈkɛxas, *eje* ˈɛxe.

(2) ɛ is used in all closed syllables,[1] excepting those where the closing consonant is đ, m, n, θ, or s.

Examples:

fuerte ˈfwɛrte, *ver* bɛr, *miel* mjɛl;

but *merced* mɛrˈθeđ, *ejemplo* ɛˈxemplo, *adentro* aˈđentro, *vez* beθ, *desdicha* deşˈđica.

Note. This rule holds good even if *e* is preceded by rr:

restoˈrresto not ˈrrɛsto,

renta ˈrrenta not ˈrrɛnta.

[1] See note on Syllabification, § 60 ff.

(3) e is the first element of the diphthongs written *eo* (eǫ) and *eu* (ey); ɛ is the first element of the diphthong written *ei* or *ey* (ɛi̯).

36. EXERCISES:

(*a*) Practise e long, then short. Alternate with English eɪ and English ɛ.

(*b*) Read out several times:

pe, be, te, de, etc.

ep, eb, et, ed, etc.

quede ˈkeđe, *erré* eˈrre, *pesebre* peˈseɓre, *jirel* xiˈrel, *medré* meˈđre, *vigente* biˈxente, *célebre* ˈθeleɓre, *reír* rreˈir, *erguir* erˈgir, *Elche* ˈelce.

(*c*) Contrast, reading aloud:

English		Spanish	
say	seɪ	*sé*	se
disdain	dɪsˈdeɪn	*desdén*	deşˈđen
mess	mes ⎫	*mes*	mes
mace	meis ⎭		
rays	reɪz	*reyes*	ˈrrejes
permit	pəˈmɪt	*permitir*	permiˈtir

a

37. EXAMPLES: *ajuar* aˈxwar, *atalaya* ataˈlaja, *baja* ˈbaxa, *igual* iˈgwal, *delante* deˈlante, *lástima* ˈlastima, *Generalife* xeneraˈlife, *calle* ˈkaʎe, *paz* paθ, *sábana* ˈsaɓana, *prado* ˈprađo.

38. DESCRIPTION: The front of the tongue is not raised, but remains in an open position. The lips are wide apart. The soft palate is raised.

39. ARTICULATION: The English tendency is to substitute for a, either æ or ɑ, according to which vowel-sound would be

used if the word were English. For instance, *paz* will be pronounced **pæθ** instead of **paθ**, and *mano* will be **ˈmanoʊ** instead of **ˈmano**. Cockneys sometimes use the Spanish vowel when they say *cup*, and Northerners often use it for words like *bath*, *castle*, etc. To learn the sound, the pupil must begin with **æ** and make it more like **a**, or vice versa. With careful guidance, the vowel may be learned very quickly.

40. **Unstressed a.** This must be as well articulated as when stressed: *catalana* **kataˈlana**, *algarabía* **algaraˈbia**.

41. **Back a.** a is articulated farther back in certain cases. This is not usually shown in transcription, but for narrow transcription the symbol **ɑ** is used. The difference between a and ɑ in Spanish is not very great, and not nearly so marked as in French. Generally speaking, when *a* is stressed and followed by **x**, the back a is used:

Tajo **ˈtaxo**, *página* **ˈpaxina** but *ajedrez* **axeˈðreθ**.

ɑ is used in the diphthongs written *ao* and *au* (**ɑǫ, ɑụ**). ɑ is also used, and lengthened (**ɑː**), in exclamations where in normal speech a would be used:

¡En el nombre del Santísimo Padre!...¡Piedad!
en el **ˈnombre ðel sanˈtisimo ‖paðre   pjeˈðɑː**

42. Dialectically, **ɑ** is heard in other positions. "In the popular speech the tendency to use **ɑ** is more general than in educated speech. Abuse of this sound is usually ascribed, according to the individual, either to ignorance or to affectation" (T. Navarro Tomás, *Manual de Pronunciación Española*).

43. EXERCISES:

(*a*) Practise a long, then short. Alternate with English æ and English ɑ.

(b) Read out several times:

pa, ba, ta, da, etc.

ap, ab, at, ad, etc.

cada ˈkaða, *alas* ˈalas, *hasta* ˈasta, *ágil* ˈaxil, *Baltasar* baltaˈsar, *alcázar* alˈkaθar, *alelí* aleˈli, *santa* ˈsanta, *jabalí* xaβaˈli, *cid Hamete Benengeli* θið aˈmete βenenˈxeli.

(c) Contrast, reading aloud:

English		Spanish	
Trafalgar	trəˈfælgə	*Trafalgar*	trafalˈgar
Gibraltar	dʒɪˈbrɔltə	*Gibraltar*	xiβralˈtar
plan	plæn	*plan*	plan
apart	əˈpɑt	*aparte*	aˈparte
mast	mɑst	*mastil*	masˈtil

CHAPTER IV

BACK VOWELS

44. There are two back vowels in Spanish, **o** and **u**. Like the front vowels they do not occur in English and must not

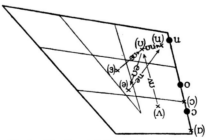

Diagram No. 6. The Spanish Back Vowels and the vowel-sounds substituted for them by English learners
( ) denote English vowels

be confused with the English vowel-sounds, which are represented the same way in orthography.

o

45. EXAMPLES: *coche* 'koce, *oro* 'oro, *codo* 'koᵭo, *comprar* kom'prar, *con* kon, *coger* ko'xer, *ojalá* oxa'la, *rosa* 'rrosa, *morisco* mo'risko, *corro* 'korro.

46. DESCRIPTION: The back of the tongue is raised to a position about half-way between the positions for an open and for a close back vowel (compare with e). There is a close lip-rounding. The soft palate is raised.

47. ARTICULATION: The usual English vowel-sound substituted for o does not approach the position of o at all. It varies from ɜʊ to ʌʊ (see diagram). ɜ is the vowel-sound in *earth*, ʊ is the vowel-sound in *put*, and ʌ is heard in *cup*. Scottish speakers use a vowel very like the Spanish vowel, but it is closer, nearer the French. To learn o, begin with the English ɔ (as in *wall*), add a close lip-rounding, and modify the sound very slightly to o, by making it more like u (as in *pool*). The vowel o is fairly easy to learn if it is remembered that it has nothing at all in common with the English diphthong. As with all vowels, the student must be careful to use o when speaking Spanish, and not to keep it for use in isolation only. *Monótono* is pronounced mo'notono, not mə'nɒtɜnoʊ. For the open o (see below), the student must use an open lip-rounding and make his o more like the English ɒ (as in *dog*). It is important to use the correct lip-rounding. Open lip-rounding means that the lips are protruded, forming a fairly large oval, unlike close lip-rounding, where there is only room for the insertion of the little finger between the lips. Open lip-rounding is sometimes called trumpet lip-rounding. Lip-rounding is essential in Spanish, though it is not so exaggerated as in French.

48. Open **o**. As for open **e**, there is a symbol for open **o** (ɔ), which is only used for narrow transcription. These are the rules for the use of ɔ and **o**:

49. (1) If *o* is preceded or followed by **rr**, it is pronounced ɔ.

Examples: *borrar* bɔˈrrar, *corre* ˈkɔrre, *rosa* ˈrrɔsa, *arroyo* aˈrrɔjo.

(2) ɔ is used before **x**.

Examples: *coger* kɔˈxer, *ojeriza* ɔxeˈriθa.

(3) ɔ is used in all closed syllables,[1] excepting those in which the closing consonant is **s**.

Examples: *corto* ˈkɔrto, *poltrón* pɔlˈtrɔn, *galardón* galarˈdɔn, *coz* kɔθ,

but *dos* dos, *amos* ˈamos.

(4) In all other circumstances **o** is used: i.e. in all open syllables unless excluded by the foregoing rules.

Examples: *pozo* ˈpoθo, *hoyo* ˈojo, *ahora* aˈora, *cobre* ˈkoƀre.

(5) ɔ is the first element of the diphthong written *oi* or *oy* (ɔi̯).

50. Some Spaniards use ɔ in many other positions, particularly when singing: but it is not Castilian to do so in ordinary conversation.

51. EXERCISES:

(*a*) Practise **o** long, then short. Alternate with English ɔ.

(*b*) Read out several times:

po, bo, to, do, etc.

op, ob, ot, od, etc.

monte ˈmonte, *torero* toˈrero, *señora* seˈɲora, *color* koˈlor, *pomo* ˈpomo, *olla podrida* ˈoʎa poˈdrida, *amapola* amaˈpola, *arrebol* arreˈƀol.

---

[1] See note on Syllabification, § 60 ff.

(*c*) Contrast, reading aloud:

English		Spanish	
court	kɔt	*corte*	ˈkorte
confess	knˈfɛs	*confieso*	komˈfjeso
ion	ˈaɪən	*ion*	jon
loco	ˈloʊkoʊ	*loco*	ˈloko
tone	toʊn	*tono*	ˈtono

u

52. EXAMPLES: *uno* ˈuno, *tribu* ˈtriƀu, *churro* ˈcurro, *húmedo* ˈumeɗo, *baúl* baˈul, *puro* ˈpuro, *chufa* ˈcufa, *abur* aˈƀur, *estuche* esˈtuce, *pantuflo* panˈtuflo.

53. DESCRIPTION: The back of the tongue is raised to a very close position. There is a close lip-rounding. Energy must be used. The soft palate is raised.

54. ARTICULATION: The English learner will probably substitute for u one of the three English vowel-sounds shown on the diagram, i.e. u as in *pool*, ʊ as in *pull*, or ʊə as in *sure*. The Spanish vowel u is a pure vowel and must be so pronounced, even when it precedes an r. Instead of u, some English people use ʊu or əu; these sounds must not, of course, be used in Spanish. To avoid making them, the pupil should lengthen the vowel-sound which he normally uses and articulate it with great energy, at the same time trying to raise the back of the tongue. u is an easy vowel to learn, for if the pupil says an English u, energetically and with close lip-rounding, he will be articulating a good Spanish u, the energy serving to raise the tongue to the required position.

55. EXERCISES:

(*a*) Practise u long, then short.

(b) Read out several times:

pu, bu, tu, du, etc.

up, ub, ut, ud, etc.

cartucho kar'tuco, *sucio* 'suθjo, *cucharada* kuca'raða, *justicia* xus'tiθja, *naturaleza* natura'leθa, *Asturias* as-'turjas, *luna* 'luna.

(c) Contrast, reading aloud:

English		Spanish	
natural	'nætʃərɫ	*natural*	natu'ral
pure	pjʊə	*puro*	'puro
duke	djʊuk or djuk	*duque*	'duke
moor	mʊə	*muralla*	mu'raʎa
mute	mjut	*mudo*	'muðo

CHAPTER V

ADDITIONAL NOTES ON VOWELS

56. DIPHTHONGS. We have already observed that a diphthong moves from one vowel-sound to another (§ 22). These sounds occur in isolation as pure vowels. Not all languages contain diphthongs. There are nine in educated southern English, but French has none at all. In Spanish there are eight diphthongs, of which four, ei̯, ai̯, ɔi̯ and au̯, are frequently used, and four others, eo̯, eu̯, ou̯ and ao̯, which occur rarely. Other diphthongs of all kinds are formed in connected speech. Orthographically, a stressed diphthong is shown (when necessary) by an accent over the *first* letter of the diphthong: an accent over the *second* letter shows that the two vowels are

in *hiatus* and do not form a diphthong, since they are pronounced separately.

EXAMPLES:

cantáis kan'taįs, *perdéis* per'ðɛįs;

but *ahí* a'i, *creí* kre'i.

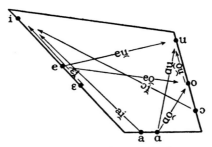

Diagram No. 7. The Spanish Diphthongs

57. ɛį, aį, ɔį and aų. ɛį must not be pronounced eɪ, as in *day*, and aį must not be pronounced aɪ, as in *eye*. Similarly, ɔį must be pronounced differently from ɔɪ, as in *boy*, and aų must not be confused with aʊ, as in *how*. These mistakes can be easily avoided by articulating the diphthongs with energy, and remembering they are made up of Spanish vowels.

58. oų must be distinguished from oʊ, as in *go*. eǫ, eų and aǫ are not likely to be confused with English diphthongs.

59. EXERCISES:

(*a*) Practise the diphthongs after consonants.

(*b*) Read out several times:

rey rrɛį, *peine* 'pɛįne, *veis* bɛįs, *hay* aį, *aire* 'aįre, *paisaje* paį'saxe, *hoy* ɔį, *estoy* es'tɔį, *convoy* kom'bɔį, *aunque* 'aųŋke, *sauce* 'saųθe, *aullar* aų'ʎar, *beodo* 'beǫðo, *europeo* eu̯roˈpeǫ, *deuda* ˈdeu̯da, *caoba* ˈkaǫba, *Bilbao* bilˈbaǫ, *bou*[1] bou̯, *Douro* ˈdou̯ro.

60. SYLLABIFICATION. When a syllable ends with a vowel, it is said to be an *open syllable.* If the syllable ends with a consonant, it is said to be a *closed syllable.*

Example: *haber* aˈber is divided a-ber, the first syllable being open and the second closed.

61. If possible, a syllable must begin with a consonant in Spanish. *h* is not a consonant, since it is never pronounced. In dividing a Spanish word into syllables, the following rules must be observed:

62. (1) When two vowels are separated by a single consonant (including *rr, ll* and *ch*), or by one of the following groups, *pr, br, tr, dr, cr, gr, fr, pl, bl, cl, gl, fl,* the first vowel is left in an open syllable and the consonant, or consonantal group, joins with the second vowel to form part, or the whole, of the following syllable.

Examples: *casa* ka-sa, *amenaza* a-me-na-θa, *inhumano* i-nu-ma-no, *cebolla* θe-bo-ʎa, *parral* pa-rral, *capricho* ka-pri-co, *cobre* ko-bre, *otro* o-tro, *ladrón* la-dron, *sacrificio* sa-kri-fi-θjo, *vinagre* bi-na-gre, *cofre* ko-fre, *soplo* so-plo, *retablo* rre-ta-blo, *oclusiva* o-klu-si-ba, *iglesia* i-gle-sja, *pantuflo* pan-tu-flo.

(2) When two vowels are separated by two consonants not forming one of the above groups, or by a consonant plus one of the above groups, the first consonant is retained to close the first syllable.

[1] "Con este diptongo no hay otra voz castellana. Las que solemos oír en la conversación y pasan a los libros, o son geográficas, o pertenecen a otras lenguas; como *Alfou, Nou, Roure,* etcétera, en Cataluña; *ou* (o), *ouido* (oído), *ouro* (oro), *Couso, Louro, Mourazos,* etc., en Galicia; *Alcoutim, Bouro, Couto, Gouvea, Louredo, Sousa, Vouga,* etc., en Portugal." (*Gramática de la Lengua Española,* p. 453; Madrid: Academia Española, 1931. 9th ed.)

Examples: *acto* **ak-to,** *alto* **al-to,** *corta* **kor-ta,** *cesta* **θes-ta,** *manga* **maŋ-ga,** *concha* **kon-ca,** *poltrón* **pol-tron,** *liendre* **ljen-dre,** *tiemblo* **tjem-blo.**

(3) Syllables can only begin with single consonants or one of the above groups. All other groups must be divided.

Examples: *ofuscar* **o-fus-kar,** *conspirar* **kons-pi-rar,** *construyó* **kons-tru-jo.**

(4) The semi-vowels **j** and **w** are not considered as consonants unless they stand alone intervocalically or initially.

Examples: *agua* **a-gwa,** *Talia* **ta-lja,** *aya* **a-ja,** *ahuecar* **a-we-kar,** *hueso* **we-so.**

63. It is essential to understand Spanish syllabification because it is often the deciding factor in determining the use of open *e* and open *o*. It is a good plan to test your knowledge by transcribing a short passage of Spanish, and dividing up the syllables as shown in the example above.

64. VOWEL SEQUENCES. When considering the movements of the vocal cords, we noticed the formation of a consonant called the glottal stop, caused by a plosion in the glottis. In English this is frequently used before an initial vowel.

Examples:

I don't know.	‖ʔai doʊnt noʊ.
I'll come, anyhow.	¹ʔail kʌm, ¹ʔɛnɪhaʊ.

65. In many dialects of English, such as Cockney, the glottal stop is used in many other circumstances as well.

Example:

Have you got any butter?   æv jə ¹gɒʔ ənɪ ¹bʌʔə.

66. There is no glottal stop in Spanish, and the English learner must be careful not to use it. Thus *alma* is ¹alma not ¹ʔalma. One of the occasions when the glottal stop can be

most easily avoided is when an initial vowel follows a final consonant, as in *un amigo*. The student should consider this as all one phrase—*unamigo*. When this phrase is divided into syllables, there will be no tendency to insert a glottal stop before *amigo* (?aˈmigo), since *a* is part of the syllable **na, u-na-mi-go**. In transcribing Spanish, however, words are kept separate, as in the language, to help reading. *Un amigo* would therefore be transcribed **un aˈmigo**. But it is suggested that the learner should always, until he has mastered the difficulty, help his pronunciation by placing a linking-mark ‿ under the final consonant and initial vowel, to remind him that they really form part of the same syllable.

Examples: *un amigo* **uˈn‿amigo**, *dos hombres* **doˈs‿ombres**.

67. Similarly, the glottal stop must not be used between two vowels: *se acabó* **se‿akaˈβo** not se ?akaˈβo.

This will be shown more clearly in the examples below.

68. In pronunciation, Spanish always tends to reduce syllables which contain a sequence of two or more vowels.

69. (*a*) ELISION. When two vowels of the same nature are found together, they are pronounced as one. If they occur within the same word they are transcribed with only one symbol; if they occur at the end of one word and the beginning of the next they are both represented, but a bracket is placed underneath to show that they are part of the same syllable and therefore pronounced as one vowel. The process of combining two vowels of the same nature into one syllable is called *elision*.

Examples:

azahar **aˈθar**, *poseedor* **poseˈdor**, *lo original* **lo‿orixiˈnal**,

la anciana **la‿anˈθjana**, *la arena azul* **la‿aˈrena‿aˈθul**

(in syllables the last phrase would be **la-re-na-θul**).

There are certain exceptions to this rule:

(1) Both vowels are pronounced in slow or careful speech.

(2) Both vowels are usually pronounced in the following words: *creencia* kreˈenθja, *mohoso* moˈoso, *loor* loˈor, *creer* and *leer* (when final, as *no quiero leer* no ˈkjero leˈer), and verbs whose stem ends in *e*, when followed by a verbal ending beginning in *e* (e.g. *creedlo* kreˈeꟼlo).

(*b*) SYNALOEPHA. When two different vowels are found together, they form part of the same syllable. If the first vowel is *i* or *u*, it is pronounced as a semi-vowel and transcribed **j** or **w** respectively. When the two vowels are found in the same word and do not form either a diphthong or a semi-vowel and vowel, they are each marked with the sign ⌢ underneath, to show they form part of the same syllable. If the syllable is stressed, as in *teatro*, the vowel which would normally be stressed in slow pronunciation is not marked with the symbol ⌢, since it is the stronger vowel. When the vowels do not resolve into a semi-vowel and vowel they are joined by a linking-mark. The process of combining two different vowels into one syllable is called *synaloepha*.

Examples: *bien* bjen, *agua* ˈagwa, *peinar* pei̯ˈnar, *aullar* au̯ˈʎar, *teatral* tea̯ˈtral, *teatro* ˈtea̯tro, *pan y agua* pan ˈj agwa, *deber u obligación* deˈꞴer w oꞴligaˈθjon, *agua y pan* ˈagwa‿i ˈpan, *beba usted* ˈbeꞴa‿usˈte, *un héroe* uˈn eroe̯, *todo eso* toˈꞴo‿eso.

EXCEPTIONS:

(1) Both vowels are sometimes pronounced fully, if one of them is stressed: *estío* esˈtio or esˈtio̯, *cohete* koˈete or ˈkoe̯te.

(2) *Ahora*, *ahí* and *aún* are pronounced ˈao̯ra, ai̯ and au̯n when they are in an unimportant position.

Example: *ahí está* ai̯ esˈta (or ajesˈta).

(3) The orthographical accent is disregarded in the following examples: *flúido* ¹flwiđo, *período* pe¹rjođo, *etíope* e¹tjope, *-íaco* -jako (as in *cardíaco*), and a few others.

(c) In all other cases, a sequence of vowels is reduced to the smallest number of syllables.

Examples:

averiguáis	ađeri¹gwais̜,
despreciéis	despre¹θjɛis̜,
¡si hoy estuviera aquí!	¹sj‿ɔi̜ estu¹đjera‿aki,
iba a Austria	i¹ḃa‿a‿au̜strja.

70. It is impossible to make fixed rules for elision, synaloepha and hiatus. This fact is attested by Spanish poetry, in which examples may be found of words being sometimes pronounced with hiatus and sometimes without it: this not infrequently occurs in the same poem.

71. NASAL VOWELS. The student will have noticed that in the articulation of the vowels, the soft palate is raised. If the soft palate is lowered, so that the air-stream can go out through the nasal cavity, as well as through the mouth, the speaker is articulating a *nasal vowel* (see Diagram No. 2). The importance of nasal vowels in French and Portuguese is due to their being a significant element of the language and used for distinguishing words. Spanish nasal vowels are not important. They are only used when a vowel is in proximity to a nasal consonant, and would not be noticed in slow or careful speech. Nasal vowels are not usually marked in phonetic transcription, but in narrow transcription they might be written ĩ, ẽ, ã, etc.

Examples: *niño* ¹nĩɲo, *mostrenco* mos¹trẽŋko, *maña* ¹mãɲa, *ronco* ¹rrɔ̃ŋko, *nunca* ¹nũŋka.

72. EXERCISES ON VOWELS.

Note. In these exercises the student should pay no attention to the consonants. Open e and open o are shown as ɛ and ɔ. Initial vowels are joined by a linking-mark to preceding consonants.

(1) Read out:

    (*a*) la le̯aˑlˈtaʤ ʤɛl‿alˈkai̯ʤe ʎeˈgo‿a loˈs‿oiʤoş ʤɛl ˈrrɛi̯.

    (*b*) ˈdoθeˈle̯ones ˈpwestos‿en ˈrrweʤa‿an daʤo ˈnombre‿al ˈpatjo.

    (*c*) no ˈai̯, tal ˈβeθ, niŋˈguna ˈkaʎe‿eu̯roˈpea̯ ˈkujo moβiˈmjento ˈsea tan‿inˈtenso‿i ˈtaŋ konˈtinwo.

    (*d*) en loş ʤoˈmiŋgos‿i ˈfjestaş ʤe ˈsantoş βalenˈθjanos, apareˈθia la‿u̯ˈme̯ante ˈpa̯eʎa.

    (*e*) ˈesta θjuˈʤaʤ ʤe los ˈsweɲos, ni ˈmwɛrta komo ˈβruxas nj‿en‿eskeˈleto komo pɔmˈpeja‿es, sin‿emˈbargo, una θjuˈʤaʤ jaˈθente, ʤɔrˈmiʤa‿a la ˈβera ʤɛl ˈtaxo, a la ˈsɔmbra ʤe ˈpjeʤraş lɛxenˈdarjas.

(2) Read out and transcribe the vowels in the following passage:

La escena parece un grabado de Durero; hay en ella una ansiedad, un misterio, una melancolía, una vaga inquietud que nos estremece el espíritu. Una dama—disfrazada de varón— anda descarriada por un monte; la acompaña un fiel escudero. Al dar vuelta a un recodo del vericueto descubren una salida torre; son los últimos momentos del crepúsculo vespertino; se inflama el cielo con los resplandores de un ocaso sangriento; una nube de nácar acaso camina lentamente hacia Oriente. Desde lo alto del lomazo que los viajeros acaban de dejar, se divisa, allá en la remota lontananza, por un gollizo abierto entre las montañas, la confusa masa de una gran ciudad.

AZORÍN.

CHAPTER VI

PLOSIVE CONSONANTS

73. In articulating a *plosive consonant*, the passage of the air-stream is blocked completely at some point, and then released, causing a *plosion*. We have already studied one plosive consonant, the glottal stop. There are eight plosive[1] consonants in Spanish—p, b, t, d, c, ɟ, k and g.

p, t and k

74. EXAMPLES: *poco* ˈpoko, *topar* toˈpar, *campo* ˈkampo, *toque* ˈtoke, *horchata* orˈcata, *quita* ˈkita, *estanque* esˈtaŋke, *patria* ˈpatrja, *acre* ˈakre, *apretar* apreˈtar.

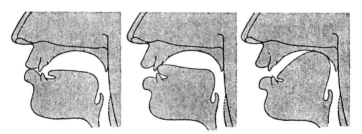

Diagram No. 8. Spanish **p, t, k** and **b, d, g**

p and **b**   **t** and **d**   **k** and **g**

75. **p, t** and **k** are all voiceless, i.e. there is no vibration of the vocal cords. The soft palate is raised.

76. **p** is made by closing the lips together. The manner and

---

[1] Properly, c and ɟ are *affricates*; but it is convenient in the case of Spanish to treat them together with the plosive consonants.

place of articulation are the same as for *p* in English, apart from aspiration (see § 80). p is a bilabial consonant.

77. t is made by touching the upper teeth with the tip of the tongue. In English, we have an alveolar *t*, i.e. the tip of the tongue touches the alveolar ridge. At first, it is very difficult for learners to avoid using an English *t* in Spanish, as the difference in sound is not usually perceptible to an untrained ear. Most people can make a dental *t* in isolation, but forget to use it in speaking Spanish. This can be remedied by constant practice. Aspiration must be avoided (see § 80). t is a dental consonant.

78. k is represented orthographically by *c* when it precedes *a, o* or *u,* and by *qu* when it precedes *i* or *e.* When *qu* precedes *a* or *o,* it is pronounced kw, like *cu.*

Examples: *cual* kwal, *quórum* ˈkworun.

79. k is made by the back of the tongue being raised until it touches the soft palate: it is therefore a velar consonant. It does not always touch the soft palate in the same place, the position it assumes for front vowels being farther forward than for the back vowels. Aspiration must be avoided.

80. ASPIRATION. In English, the voiceless plosive consonants p, t, k are *aspirated.* Their articulation is immediately followed by a puff of air. In Spanish there is no aspiration at all. p, t and k should be carefully practised before vowels, and not pronounced with too much energy.

81. In the following diagram, the English word *pity* and the Spanish word *pata* have been compared, to show how the English consonants are aspirated—ˈpʰɪtʰɪ. The horizontal line indicates when the vocal cords are vibrating (during the articulation of the vowels). It will be seen that in English

there is a gap between consonant and vowel, while the Spanish vowels follow on immediately.

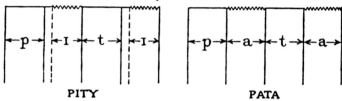

PITY   PATA

Diagram No. 9. Aspiration in English

82. If the student is unable to make p, t and k unaspirated, he should make them more like initial English b, d and g, which are much more like the Spanish p, t and k, than are the aspirated p, t and k.

b, d and g

83. EXAMPLES: *banco* ˈbaŋko, *blancura* blaŋˈkura, *ambos* ˈambos, *enviar* emˈbjar, *voy* bɔi̯, *doy* dɔi̯, *diente* ˈdjente, *anda* ˈanda, *espaldas* esˈpaldas, *goma* ˈgoma, *grabar* graˈƀar, *tengo* ˈteŋgo, *manga* ˈmaŋga.

84. b, d and g are all voiced consonants. The soft palate is raised. These consonants are exactly the same as p, t and k respectively, excepting that they are fully voiced.

85. b is represented orthographically by *b* and *v*. When either of these letters is at the beginning of a sentence, it is pronounced b. *b* and *v* are also pronounced b if they are preceded by *m* or *n*. English learners do not always pronounce *v* correctly, and it should be remembered that in *no position at all* has *v* anything like the sound it has in English. b is a bilabial consonant.

86. d is a dental consonant, unlike *d* in English, which is alveolar. d is used in Spanish, when *d* is at the beginning of a sentence, and also when *d* is preceded by *l* or *n*.

87. g is represented orthographically by *g* when it precedes *a, o* or *u,* and by *gu* when it precedes *i* or *e;* in these cases *g* (or *gu*) must be at the beginning of a sentence or following *n.* If *gu* precedes *a* or *o,* and is initial or preceded by *n,* it is pronounced **gw.**

Examples: *Guillermo* giˡʎermo, *guante* ˡgwante.

88. g is a velar consonant; the exact place of articulation varies, like **k.**

89. VOICING. b, d and g are all fully voiced.[1] In English, *b, d* and *g* are not always voiced; they are often not voiced when they occur in initial and final positions. The Spanish consonants must be fully voiced, otherwise they will sound like p, t and k to a Spaniard. For instance, *basta* pronounced with an English b sounds like *pasta* to a Spaniard (it does not to an Englishman, because p in English is aspirated, cf. §§ 80–82). Lack of voicing in English b is illustrated in the following diagram.

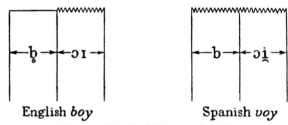

English *boy*   Spanish *voy*

Diagram No. 10. Voicing in Spanish

90. Practically, there is little difference between an initial English *b* and a Spanish *p.* But the difference does exist. It requires more effort to say a p than it does to say a voiceless

---

[1] Although they are fully voiced, they must not be articulated with such *energy* as the French voiced plosives.

b (ƀ). This cannot be shown on a diagram like the one above, but it is a fact which the reader can easily verify, by comparing the two words *bad* and *pata*: the difference can only be shown on a kymographic tracing. All this applies equally to d and g.

91. Many English people find it very hard to make a fully voiced plosive. The point to remember is that the vocal cords must vibrate, all the time the organs of speech are in position for articulating b, d or g. The best way to learn b, d and g is to learn the corresponding fricatives ƀ, đ and g first (see Chapter IX). Let us take b. Produce voice by articulating a vowel and holding it on. Gradually bring the lips together until friction is heard, and then gently close the lips. The plosion caused by closing and opening the lips will be a fully voiced b. The same process should be tried with d, bringing the tip of the tongue against the upper teeth, and with g, bringing the back of the tongue against the soft palate.

c and ɟ

92. EXAMPLES: *charla* ˈcarla, *hacha* ˈaca, *ancho* ˈanco, *chopo* ˈcopo, *hielo* ˈɟelo, *yo* ɟo, *ya* ɟa, *cónyuge* ˈkonɟuxe.

93. c and ɟ are made by the blade of the tongue touching the alveolar ridge and part of the hard palate; for this reason, they are sometimes called post-alveolar or pre-palatal. c is voiceless and ɟ is voiced. They are usually classified as affricates, i.e. a plosive + a fricative (t+ʃ, d+ʒ). tʃ in English (as in *church* tʃɜtʃ) is a kind of t pronounced with rather slow separation of the articulating organs, so that a kind of ʃ (cf. *sh* in *ash*) is audible as the tongue is removed. Many people regard English tʃ as a "single sound". The Spanish c is also an affricate, in the opinion of many phoneticians; but it is convenient to treat it

as a single sound, and is accordingly transcribed in this book
with one symbol (c). Thus *coche* is transcribed ꞌkoce not ꞌkotʃe.

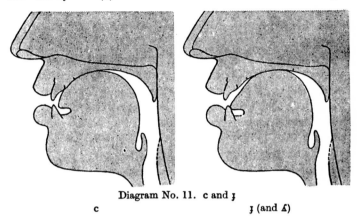

Diagram No. 11. c and ʝ

c   ʝ (and ʎ)

94. c and ʝ are fairly easy to learn. The student should not
touch the alveolar ridge with the tip of the tongue, only with
the blade of it. If he finds this difficult, he should press the
sides of the tongue against the side teeth, thus forcing the tip
down a little and making the consonant easier to say.

95. c is always represented as *ch* orthographically.

96. Use of ʝ. ʝ, which must be fully voiced, is used very
little. It is usually employed when it is desired to stress em-
phatically an initial j (the pronunciation of *y* or *hi* when
preceding a vowel). ʝ is also used usually, when initial *y* or
hi (when followed by a vowel) is preceded by final *n* or *l*:
sometimes even in the same word.

Examples:

ya ha llegado	ꞌꞌʝa‿a ʎeꞌgaðo,
la canción del yunque	la kanꞌθjon del ꞌʝuŋke,
enyuntar	enʝunꞌtar.

97. Exercises on the plosive consonants.

(*a*) Practise the plosive consonants in front of every vowel, remembering

    1. To avoid aspiration in p, t and k.

    2. To give full voicing to b, d and g.

    3. That t and d are dental consonants.

(*b*) Read out:

pulpo ˈpulpo, *tonto* ˈtonto, *pronto* ˈpronto, *postal* posˈtal, *estampa* esˈtampa, *conde* ˈkonde, *cuyo* ˈkujo, *quepo* ˈkepo, *cuatro* ˈkwatro, *cuero* ˈkwero, *convento* komˈbento, *combinar* kombiˈnar, *vamos* ˈbamos, *caldo* ˈkaldo, *andando* anˈdando, *gato* ˈgato, *mengua* ˈmeŋgwa, *dengue* ˈdeŋge, *antorcha* anˈtorca, *puchero* puˈcero, *hielo* ˈjelo.

(*c*) Read out and transcribe (as far as possible):

    1. Conchita se ha marchado.

    2. Quien canta, sus penas espanta.

    3. Busco la carta que me envió mi tío.

    4. Yo saldré ahora mismo de esta aldea.

    5. Este monte, distante dos leguas y media de Nápoles hacia la parte oriental, tiene de altura unas seiscientas toesas.

CHAPTER VII

NASAL CONSONANTS

98. Nasal consonants are those consonants, during the articulation of which the soft palate is lowered, to enable the air-stream to pass through the nasal cavity. There are five

nasal consonants in Spanish, m, ɱ, n, ɲ, ŋ. All the nasal consonants are voiced.

m and ɱ

99. EXAMPLES: *momia* ˈmomja, *ambos* ˈambos, *amparo* amˈparo, *envía* emˈbia, *enfermo* eɱˈfermo, *anfiteatro* aɱfi-ˈteatro.

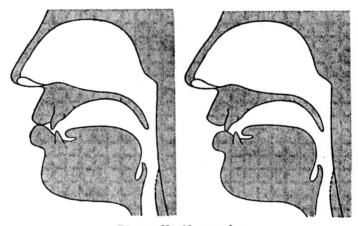

Diagram No. 12. m and ɱ

m   ɱ

100. m is a bilabial consonant like the English *m*. ɱ is labiodental: it is made by touching the upper teeth with the lower lip. ɱ is quite easy to learn, but if the student finds it difficult, he should bite his lower lip and then try to say m, without allowing his lips to meet. ɱ is used whenever *n* or *m* precedes *f* (also a labiodental consonant). The symbol ɱ is only used in narrow transcription.

101. *m* is pronounced m unless it is final or precedes *f*. m is also used whenever *n* precedes *p, b* or *v*.

Examples: *ánfora* ˈaɱfora, *en Valencia* em baˈlenθja.

n

102. EXAMPLES: *nuestro* ˈnwestro, *cana* ˈkana, *santo* ˈsanto, *blando* ˈblando, *compran* ˈkompran, *alcance* alˈkanθe, *danza* ˈdanθa, *Adán* aˈdan, *álbum* ˈalɓun, *ultimátum* ultiˈmatun.

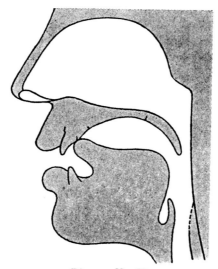

Diagram No. 13

n

103. There are three *n*'s in Spanish. The normal *n* is alveolar and is exactly like the English *n* (see Diagram No. 13). But before θ, *n* is interdental, and before t and d, *n* is dental. In other words, the tip of the tongue touches the upper teeth as

in Diagram No. 8 or No. 20, instead of touching the alveolar ridge. These three *n*'s are all transcribed with the symbol n.

104. Final *m* is always pronounced n in Spanish. The *n* of words like *inmóvil* is only heard in very slow or careful pronunciation.

Examples:

inmóvil in'moᵬil and i'moᵬil,

conmigo kon'migo and ko'migo.

ɲ

105. EXAMPLES: *caña* 'kaɲa, *señal* se'ɲal, *puñal* pu'ɲal, *niña* 'niɲa, *cenceño* θen'θeɲo, *ñam-ñam* ɲa'ɲan, *ñudo* 'ɲuᵭo.

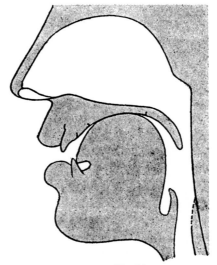

Diagram No. 14

ɲ

106. ɲ is a palatal consonant. It is not used in English but occurs in many languages as well as Spanish—French, Italian, Greek, Czech, etc. To articulate ɲ, the learner must press the tip of the tongue against the lower teeth and try to say the word *new*: by doing so he will be touching the hard palate with the front of the tongue and actually saying ɲu (instead of nju).

107. ɲ is always represented by *ñ* in orthography. The student must be careful to avoid confusion between ɲ and nj, since nj consists of two articulations, a consonant and a semivowel.

Distinguish between:

> *miño* ˈmiɲo and *minio* ˈminjo,
> *uñón* uˈɲon and *unión* uˈnjon.

ŋ

108. EXAMPLES: *enjuto* eŋˈxuto, *manga* ˈmaŋga, *tango* ˈtaŋgo, *abolengo* aβoˈleŋgo, *yunque* ˈjuŋke, *brincar* briŋkar.

109. ŋ is a velar consonant and is made by the back of the tongue touching the soft palate. ŋ is the sound of *ng* in the English word *sang*. *n* is always pronounced ŋ when it precedes one of the velar consonants k, g or x. Students must remember particularly to use ŋ before x—*enjambre* eŋˈxambre.

110. Exercises on the nasal consonants:

(a) Read out:

sin vergüenza sim berˈgwenθa, *en virtud* em birˈtuð, *un favor* uɱ faˈβor, *con braveza* kom braˈβeθa, *un par* um par, *senda* ˈsenda, *confort* koɱˈfort, *ninfa* ˈniɱfa, *harem* aˈren, *en Francia* eɱ ˈfranθja, *mano* ˈmano, *Nuño* ˈnuɲo, *baño* ˈbaɲo, *mancha*

ˈmanca, *común* koˈmun, *rango* ˈrraŋgo, *dominio* doˈminjo, *línea* ˈlinε̞a, *piña* ˈpiɲa, *ingeniero* iŋxeˈnjero.

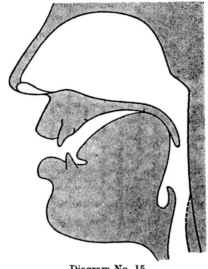

Diagram No. 15

ŋ

CHAPTER VIII

L-SOUNDS AND R-SOUNDS

l and ł

111. EXAMPLES: *luto* ˈluto, *lomo* ˈlomo, *cala* ˈkala, *pila* ˈpila, *plano* ˈplano, *igual* iˈgwal, *sol* sol, *falso* ˈfalso, *bulto* ˈbułto, *baúl* baˈuł.

112. *l* in Spanish has two sounds. They are both voiced alveolar consonants, made by putting the tip of the tongue

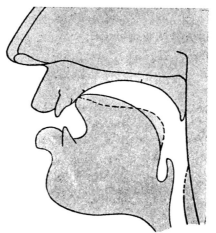

Diagram No. 16. Clear l and dark l
Dark l (ł) is shown by the dotted line

against the teeth ridge, and allowing the air to pass out at the sides of the tongue. The difference between the two *l*'s is in the position of the rest of the tongue: if it is in the position for a front vowel, the consonant will have a front-vowel resonance, this is called *clear l* (l). If the rest of the tongue is in the position for a back vowel, the *l* will have a back-vowel resonance, this is called *dark l* (ł) (see Diagram No. 16). We have both *l*'s in English, in the word *little* lɪtł. ł in Spanish is not so dark as in English and is only used after *u*, when it closes a syllable.[1]

[1] ł is also heard, not infrequently, when *l* occurs at the end of a syllable following *o* (ɔ) and *a* (ɑ), as in *bolsa* ˈbɔłsa, *igual* iˈgwɑł.

113. Like **n**, **1** suits its articulation to the following consonant, being interdental before **θ** and dental before **t** and **d**. The learner should be careful to observe this rule, as it will help considerably towards gaining a fluent pronunciation.

114. 1 and ɫ are both lateral consonants.

ʎ

115. EXAMPLES: *calle* ˈkaʎe, *olla* ˈoʎa, *llama* ˈʎama, *pollo* ˈpoʎo, *pillo* ˈpiʎo, *brillar* briˈʎar, *lleno* ˈʎeno.

116. ʎ is a voiced palatal consonant. It is made by pressing the tip of the tongue against the lower teeth and touching the hard palate with the front of the tongue.[1] It must not be confused with lj which, like **nj**, is a double articulation. ʎ is *ll* in orthography. Thus *hallarse* and *aliarse* are as distinct in pronunciation as they are in spelling, aˈʎarse and aˈljarse.

117. Use of ʎ. Not all Spaniards use ʎ. Many of them pronounce *ll* as though it were *y*, thus confusing words like *halla* and *haya* by giving them exactly the same pronunciation—ˈaja. The use of j for ʎ is not by any means confined to dialects or to uneducated speakers. Many of the best educated Castilians, particularly those who come from Madrid, use j instead of ʎ. In Spanish, this is called *yeísmo*. Many people who use j in conversation use ʎ in slow or careful speech, and for singing and oratory ʎ is considered more correct. The student is advised to use ʎ always, until he has attained a very fluent pronunciation, when he will be able to judge for himself, by observing the speech of Spaniards, whether it would be better to substitute j.

118. ʎ is a lateral consonant.

[1] See Diagram No. 11.

rr and r

119. EXAMPLES: *cara* ˈkara, *mirlo* ˈmirlo, *pera* ˈpera, *camarero* kamaˈrero, *querer* keˈrer, *brío* ˈbrio, *creyó* kreˈjo, *cobrar* koˈbrar, *roble* ˈrroble, *rey* rrɛi̯, *parral* paˈrral, *honra* ˈonrra, *alrededor* alrreðeˈðor.

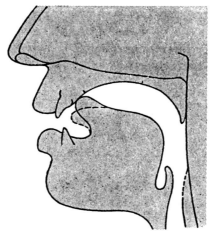

Diagram No. 17
r and rr

120. rr is a rolled alveolar consonant: it is fully voiced. Although rr is not a sound used in educated southern English, most English people can make it. Those who cannot should repeat tərətərə several times, using a dental *t* and the *r* of *very*; after a short while the tongue should vibrate. If this fails, the student should try again, using the word *thorough*. rr should never be attempted if the speaker is tired; he should be careful not to hold his tongue rigid and to practise it with strong, sudden jerks of breath.

121. Use of **rr.** **rr** is the pronunciation of *rr* and *sr* and of initial *r*; *nr* and *lr* are pronounced nrr and lrr. For the loss of *s* in *sr* see § 141. Many people think they hear a d in the group **nrr.** This is because in moving the tongue from a non-vibrant consonant to a vibrant, a plosion is caused which is in fact an alveolar d. The insertion of a d between n and r is shown in Old Spanish (*ondra* for (*h*)*onra*), and in many other languages.

122. **rr** consists of two or more vibrations, according to emphasis, and it is really a long **r,** which consists of one vibration or tap. **r** is called a flapped consonant and is the pronunciation of *r* in all circumstances, except those enumerated in the preceding paragraph. **r** should be learned in the same way as **rr,** great care being taken that there is only one tap, since the articulation of more than one may change the meaning of a word.

Example: *para* (= for) ˈpara, but *parra* (= vine) ˈparra.

123. Exercises on l-sounds and r-sounds.

(*a*) Practise 1 and **r** intervocalically—ala, ara, etc.

(*b*) Read out:

reinar rrɛiˈnar, *calamar* kalaˈmar, *azul* aˈθul, *azul y rojo* aˈθul‿i ˈrroxo, *Israel* irraˈel, *pilluelo* piˈʎwelo, *un carro caro* uŋ ˈkarro ˈkaro, *llamar* ʎaˈmar, *rallar* rraˈʎar, *árboles* ˈarβoles.

(*c*) Read out and transcribe the l- and r-sounds in the following passage:

Como recuerdo de tal época, encontramos en un corral, las ruedas y parte de la caja de un landó fabricado en París. El carruaje de gala del Califa se va desmenuzando al aire libre.

CHAPTER IX

FRICATIVE CONSONANTS

124. A fricative consonant is a consonant whose articulation is brought about by the air passage being closed, not enough to cause a plosion, but sufficiently to cause audible friction. There are ten fricative consonants in Spanish, ƀ, f, θ, ɋ, đ, s, ʂ, ç, x and g: for all of these the soft palate is raised.

ƀ, đ and g

125. EXAMPLES: *ave* ˈaƀe, *lóbrego* ˈloƀrego, *hablar* aˈƀlar, *hierba* ˈjerƀa, *calvo* ˈkalƀo, *cada* ˈkađa, *cantad* kanˈtađ, *sordo* ˈsorđo, *medrar* meˈđrar, *agua* ˈagwa, *holgar* olˈgar, *siglo* ˈsiglo, *pagué* paˈge.

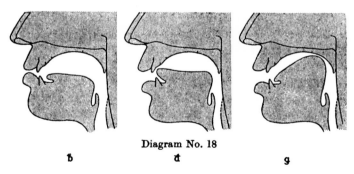

Diagram No. 18

ƀ   đ   g

126. ƀ is a bilabial consonant; it is articulated in exactly the same way as p and b, excepting that the lips do not actually touch one another throughout their whole length. ƀ is a difficult consonant for English people to learn, since they have no similar sound in their own language. The easiest way to learn it is to round the lips and sing a note, and then gradually to lessen the gap between the lips, while still singing. Another way is to whistle and then add voice. Having got so far, by one way or the other, the learner will be articulating a variety of ƀ, the ƀ which is used before u as in *tribu* (ˈtriƀu), for the lip position of ƀ anticipates the following vowel; if an i follows, the lips will be spread. In the articulation of ƀ the lower lip should be protruded; not only is this characteristic of many Spaniards, but it makes the consonant easier to pronounce, while obviating the possibility of the lower lip touching the upper teeth (as for the English *v*, a labiodental consonant). The student should be careful not to raise the upper lip, which must be brought down so as to cover the upper teeth. ƀ is fully voiced: it is easy enough to voice ƀ intervocalically, but the student must remember to give full voicing to it, when it comes in other positions as well (but compare § 128).

127. ƀ is the pronunciation of *b* and *v* unless they occur in an absolutely initial position or are preceded by *m* or *n*.

128. ƀ is pronounced voiceless when it precedes a voiceless consonant.

Examples: *absurdo* aƀ̥ˈsurɗo, *objeto* oƀ̥ˈxeto.

This voiceless ƀ (ƀ̥) changes to p in emphatic pronunciation.

Example: *absurdo* aƀ̥ˈsurɗo (normal), apˈsurɗo (emphatic).

129. ɗ. ɗ is a voiced dental consonant; it is made by a stream of air causing friction between the tip of the tongue and the upper teeth (see Diagram No. 21). In general, ɗ is the pronunciation of *d*, unless *d* is in an absolutely initial position or preceded by *n* or *l*. In the ending *-ado*, however, the ɗ is very much reduced, and is hardly audible in colloquial Spanish and familiar conversation, though it must be used in slow or correct speech for the stage, public speaking, etc.

-*ado* should always be transcribed **aᵭo**, even when it sounds like **ao**.

130. When *d* comes at the end of a group, it is normally pronounced **ᵭ**, but it is not pronounced at all in certain common words.

Examples:

> *¿Cómo está usted?* ǀkomo‿esǀta‿usǀte.
> *No quiero ir a Madrid.* no kjeǀro‿ir‿a maǀᵭri.

This *d* is of course pronounced whenever it ceases to be final. Example:

> *¿Cómo están ustedes?* ǀkomo‿esǀtan‿usǀteᵭes.

131. **ɡ.** **ɡ** is a voiced velar consonant, made by the air-stream passing between the back of the tongue and the soft palate. The best way to learn it is to practise the syllable **ɡɑ** (using the plosive **ɡ**), gradually softening the **ɡ** until the syllable flows evenly without a plosion. Students of French pronunciation may prefer to begin with the fricative uvular *r* (**ʁ**), if they can make it, and gradually move the place of articulation up the soft palate, thus making the articulation more like that of **ɡ**. If neither of these methods is successful, the student should learn **x** first (see § 147), and then add voice, at the same time lessening the friction.

132. **ɡ** is used whenever *g* (not followed by *i* or *e*) is not in an absolutely initial position or preceded by *n*.

Example: *una ganga* una ǀɡaŋɡa.

133. When *gu* is not in an absolutely initial position or preceded by *n*, it is pronounced **ɡ** before *i* or *e*, and **ɡw** before *a* or *o*.

Examples: *águila* ǀaɡila, *tregua* ǀtreɡwa.

134. Learners should be very careful to use **ƀ**, **ᵭ** and **ɡ**; neglect to do so is one of the chief faults of foreigners speaking

Spanish. Although Ƀ, đ and ǥ are fricative consonants, they should not be articulated with too much friction; they might, perhaps, be better described as consonantal glides which, when over-stressed, become plosive consonants, and when too relaxed, are lost entirely. Ƀ, đ and ǥ should be articulated very gently and smoothly.

f

135. EXAMPLES: *fuero* ˈfwero, *flamante* flaˈmante, *Francia* ˈfranθja, *sofá* soˈfa, *café* kaˈfe, *filósofo* fiˈlosofo, *infierno* iɲˈfjerno.

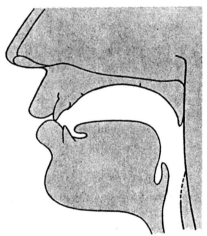

Diagram No. 19
f

136. This consonant is almost the same as English f. It is made by the lower lip lightly touching the upper teeth, and allowing the air to pass through. f is therefore a labiodental consonant, and it is voiceless. The only difference between the English and Spanish f is that there is more friction in the

Spanish consonant, owing to the greater energy which is used during articulation.

θ and ǫ

137. EXAMPLES: *cerilla* θeˈriʎa, *caza* ˈkaθa, *cinco* ˈθiŋko, *coz* koθ, *zumbido* θumˈbiɖo, *zorro* ˈθorro, *vicio* ˈbiθjo, *hallazgo* aˈʎaǫgo, *bizma* ˈbiǫma.

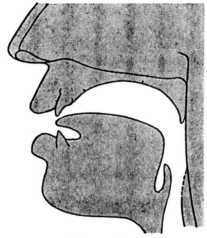

Diagram No. 20
θ and ǫ

138. θ is a voiceless interdental consonant; the tip of the tongue is held lightly against the upper teeth in an interdental position. There is much more friction in the Spanish θ than in the English θ (as heard in *th*ree). *c* before *i* and *e*, and *z* in all positions, are pronounced θ. The use of θ as the pronunciation of final *d* in words like *usted*, *verdad*, etc. is dialectal and should not be copied by foreigners speaking Spanish.

139. ẟ̧ is the voiced counterpart of θ. It is used when the phoneme precedes a voiced consonant. Voiced θ (ẟ̧) sounds rather like the English *th* of *other*. It should be noticed that ẟ̧ is quite a different sound from đ: not only is the place of articulation different (cf. Diagrams No. 18 and No. 20) but there is also more audible friction in ẟ̧.

s and ṣ

140. EXAMPLES: *soto* ꞌsoto, *casa* ꞌkasa, *rosa* ꞌrrosa, *áspid* ꞌaspiđ, *rastro* ꞌrrastro, *compás* komꞌpas, *cansado* kanꞌsađo, *asno* ꞌaṣno, *mismo* ꞌmiṣmo, *riesgo* ꞌrrjeṣgo.

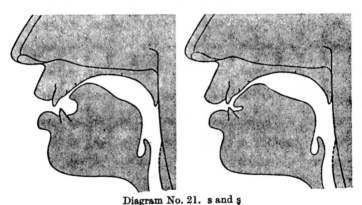

Diagram No. 21. s and ṣ

s and ṣ with the tip of the tongue raised

s and ṣ with the tip of the tongue lowered

141. s is a voiceless alveolar consonant. The tip of the tongue is raised and the air passes out through a narrow gap between the tip of the tongue and the alveolar ridge. This is the s which is used by most English people and in the greater part of Spain. The other kind of s, which is used by many

English people, and also in French, Italian, Andalusian Spanish, and in many other languages, is made by the tip of the tongue being lowered so as to allow the air-stream to pass through a gap between the blade of the tongue and the alveolar ridge. There is very little audible difference between the two varieties of s, and it is not necessary for the English learner to change his s, if it is not the same as that used in Castilian Spanish. s should be pronounced as in English, although it should never be lengthened. When final, s is articulated with less energy than usual, in quick conversation.

142. ş. s is voiced (ş) when it precedes a voiced consonant. This makes it sound like an English z. The ş itself becomes assimilated to rr when it precedes an r. Thus *dos reales*, doş ˈrreales, becomes do ˈrreales, which is better transcribed dor ˈrreales to show that the rr is rolled a little longer than usual to compensate for the lost ş. In slow or careful pronunciation *sr* is pronounced şrr or even srr.

ç

143. EXAMPLES: ¡ay! açː, ¡huy! uçː, ¡guay! gwaçː.

144. ç is a voiceless palatal consonant. To make it, the tip of the tongue is pressed against the lower teeth so that the air-stream passes through a narrow gap between the front of the tongue and the hard palate. An easy way to learn it is to say i (keeping the tip of the tongue against the lower teeth) with such force that there is audible friction; if this sound is then made voiceless it will be a ç.

145. ç is used for a final y in interjections; it is not used in any other case. It is always an alternative sound to i, and is only used when the interjection occurs alone.

Example:

¡Ay de mí! ¡Ay! ˈai̯ ᶁe ˈmi ˈˈaçː.

146. Notice that ç is usually long. Sometimes it is articulated so softly as to be almost inaudible. The student should

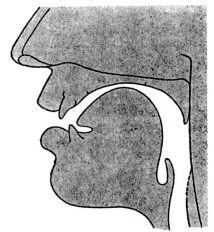

Diagram No. 22

ç

be careful not to have too much friction in his ç and to use it only on the right occasions. It is not unusual to hear Spaniards lengthen the i instead of using ç—*¡ay!* ai̯ː. Both forms are equally correct, however, and açː is certainly of more frequent occurrence.

x

147. EXAMPLES: *Jesús* xeˈsus, *jota* ˈxota, *jefe* ˈxefe, *jengibre* xeŋˈxiᵬre, *jinete* xiˈnete, *enjambre* eŋˈxambre, *ajuar* aˈxwar, *Generalife* xeneraˈlife, *Gibraltar* xiᵬralˈtar, *juzgar* xuθˈgar.

148. **x** is made by the air-stream passing between the back of the tongue and the soft palate; it is therefore a velar consonant. **x** is voiceless. English people sometimes find difficulty in pronouncing words containing **x**: this even occurs in English,

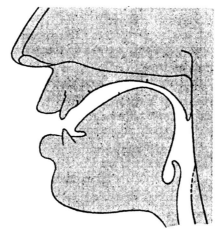

Diagram No. 23

x

loch being pronounced lɒk instead of lɒx. In other words, a plosive consonant (**k**) is used instead of the fricative. To learn **x** the student should feel with his tongue the place where **k** is articulated, and then try to force the air through at the same place. Another way to learn it is to make a voiceless **g**, and then to add more friction. Once learned, **x** will prove useful in many languages as well as Spanish.

149. **x** is the pronunciation of *g* before *e* and *i*, and of *j* in all positions.

150. Exercises on the fricative consonants.

(a) Practise ƀ, đ and ǥ between vowels—aƀa, ađa, aǥa, etc.

(b) Read out:

gobernante goƀer'nante, *medio* 'međjo, *recuerdo* rre'kwerđo, *dirigir* diri'xir, *ciego* 'θjego, *albedrío* alƀe'đrio, *todo* 'tođo, *viejo* 'bjexo, *Zocodover* θokođo'ƀer, *pedregoso* peđre'goso, *higuera* i'gera, *soledad* sole'đađ, *corbata* kor'ƀata, *objetivo* oƀxe'tiƀo, *desdén* deș'đen, *bacía* ba'θia, *acción* ak'θjon, *coger* ko'xer.

(c) Read out and transcribe phonetically:

Entre el sopor de la siesta que duerme Galicia lozana,
junto a la fuente que ronda zumbando clamante abejorro,
medio entreabierta la boca encendida, de olor a manzana,
bebe una moza las gotas del arco movible del chorro.

Y bajo d'él, colocando la herrada que trajo a la fuente,
mira llenarse la tosca vasija de inquietos albores,
como si rosas de recias espumas y luz floreciente
se desflecasen en mil carcajadas y locos temblores . . . .

SALVADOR RUEDA.

CHAPTER X

SEMI-VOWELS

151. There are two semi-vowels in Spanish, w and j. Both are voiced and the soft palate is raised during articulation.

w

152. EXAMPLES: *fuente* 'fwente, *cruel* krwel, *cuello* 'kweʎo, *ahuecar* awe'kar, *sabueso* sa'ƀweso, *huevo* 'weƀo, *huerta* 'werta, *hueste* 'weste.

153. **w** is really a glide from a very short **u** to the following vowel. If **w** is lengthened, it becomes **u**. The only difference between English and Spanish **w** is the greater energy which is needed for the Spanish semi-vowel, just as greater energy is needed for **u** in Spanish than in English.

154. **w** is both bilabial and velar (see p. xi) because the lips are rounded and the back of the tongue approaches the soft palate.

155. Use of **w**.

(i) Whenever *u* precedes a vowel-letter and is not marked with an orthographical accent, it is pronounced **w**.

Examples: *cuidar* **kwiˈdar**, *fuente* **ˈfwente**, *guapura* **gwaˈpura**, *hueste* **ˈweste**.

(ii) If *u* precedes a vowel-letter and is marked with an orthographical accent, it is pronounced **u**:

Compare *púa* **ˈpua**, *rúa* **ˈrrua**; and *suave* **ˈswaðe**, *agua* **ˈagwa**.

156. Some Spaniards use **u** instead of **w** in slow or careful speech in a few words, mostly verbal forms.

Examples:

> *huída* **ˈwiða** or **uˈiða**,
> *argüir* **arˈgwir** or **arguˈir**,
> *jesuíta* **xeˈswita** or **xesuˈita**.

j

157. EXAMPLES: *huyendo* **uˈjendo**, *yegua* **ˈjeɡwa**, *payaso* **paˈjaso**, *apoyo* **aˈpojo**, *ciento* **ˈθjento**, *agrio* **ˈaɡrjo**, *niego* **ˈnjego**, *reyes* **ˈrrejes**, *hierro* **ˈjerro**, *confiáis* **komˈfjaįs**, *escolio* **esˈkoljo**.

158. Like **w**, **j** is a glide, it glides from the position of **i** to that of the following vowel. **j** in Spanish requires more energy than in English. On occasions, particularly when it occurs

intervocalically, j is pronounced as a fricative voiced palatal consonant (the voiced counterpart of ç).

159. Initial j is sometimes pronounced ʝ (see § 96). In words which end with a diphthong, the final i̯ becomes j instead of forming the second part of a diphthong, when a vowel is added.

Examples: *buey* bwɛi̯, *bueyes* ˈbwejes, *convoy* komˈbɔi̯, *convoyes* komˈbojes.

160. Some Spaniards retain the diphthong in the plural, the *y* not being articulated with sufficient energy to separate the vowels.

Examples: *buey* bwɛi̯, *bueyes* ˈbwɛi̯es.

161. The letter *i* is sometimes pronounced i in a few words, where j might be expected.

Examples: *brioso* briˈoso (compare *brío* ˈbrio), *crianza* kriˈanθa (compare *cría* ˈkria).

Even so synaeresis (use of j instead of i, thus avoiding hiatus in these words) is frequent.

162. The letter *i*, when followed by a vowel-letter, is always pronounced j unless it is marked with an orthographical accent.

Examples: *fiel* fjel, *medio* ˈmeᵭjo, *hacia* ˈaθja, *hacía* aˈθia.

163. Exercise on the semi-vowels.

Read out and transcribe:

cuero, cambiáis, vergüenza, reyes, apariencia, frambuesa, hicieron, descendió, suerte, puente, frío, porfiar, pronunciación, feria, ahuehuete, creyera, griego, Noruega, frecuencia, criollo, cabriola.

CHAPTER XI

ADDITIONAL NOTES ON CONSONANTS

164. Pronunciation of the letter *x*. *x* before a consonant is pronounced s.

Examples: *extranjero* estraŋˈxero, *excusar* eskuˈsar.

Between vowels, *x* is pronounced ks or gs.

Examples: *examen* ekˈsamen or egˈsamen, *eximio* ekˈsimjo or egˈsimjo.

Exceptions: *exacto* eˈsakto, *auxilio* au̯ˈsiljo, *auxiliar* au̯siˈljar.

Final *x* is pronounced **x**.

Examples: *Sax* sax, *Barrax* baˈrrax.

Note. The prefix *ex-* is usually pronounced **eks**: *ex-rey* eksˈrɛi̯, *ex-ministro* eksmiˈnistro.

165. Pronunciation of the letter *g*. *g* has three pronunciations **x**, **g** and **g**.

Examples: *coge* ˈkoxe, *pongo* ˈpoŋgo, *haga* ˈaga.

g is always pronounced **x** if it precedes *e* or *i*. If *gu* precedes *e* or *i* it is pronounced g (or g).

Examples: *sanguíneo* saŋˈgineo, *albogue* alˈβoge.

If *gu* precedes *a* or *o* it is pronounced **gw** (or **gw**); this sound is spelt *gü* before *e* or *i*.

Examples: *guapo* ˈgwapo, *apacigüe* apaˈθigwe.

166. Pronunciation of the letter *c*. *c* is pronounced θ before *e* and *i*; in all other cases it is pronounced **k**.

Examples: *cielo* ˈθjelo, *cera* ˈθera, *cola* ˈkola, *cara* ˈkara.

When **k** is followed by *i* or *e*, it is spelt *qu*.

Examples: *que* ke, *quilate* kiˈlate.

167. *h*. This letter is never pronounced, except in dialects. *ch* is treated as a separate letter in the Spanish alphabet.

168. *z* and *j*. *z* is always pronounced θ, and *j* is always pronounced **x**.

Examples: *zapato* θaˈpato, *zendo* ˈθendo, *jalea* xaˈlea, *jerigonza* xeriˈgonθa.

169. *b*, *d* and *g*. In addition to when they follow certain consonants,[1] *b*, *d* and *g* are pronounced as plosives when they occur in an absolutely initial position; that is, when they begin a sentence, or a new phrase after a pause. Otherwise, although they are at the beginning of a word, they must be pronounced as fricatives (unless they are following the special consonants[1]).

Examples:

Bueno. Yo me voy.   ˈbweno ˈʝo me ˈɓɔi̯ (not bɔi̯).

¿Dónde está mi guante? ˈdonde‿esˈta mi ˈgwante (not gwante).

170. Consonants are pronounced in sentences in the same way as in words. That is to say, a consonant like *m* or *n* which is pronounced ɱ when it occurs in a word followed by *f*, has the same pronunciation if it occurs at the end of a word and is immediately followed by another word beginning with *f*.

Examples: *enfermo* eɱˈfermo, *un favor* uɱ faˈɓor, *convidar* kombiˈdar, *sin valor* sim baˈlor, *desdén* deṣˈden, *los dueños* loṣ ˈdweɲos, *gozne* ˈgoθne, *voz baja* boθ ˈɓaxa.

171. Irregular pronunciations. In addition to one or two words already mentioned, a few words do not follow the general rules for pronunciation. These are some of them: *reloj* rrɛˈlo, *cinc* θiŋ, *istmo* ˈismo, *psicología* sikoloˈxia.

b is not pronounced in the following words and their derivatives: *obscuro* osˈkuro, *substraer* susˈtraer, *subscribir* suskriˈɓir, *substancia* susˈtanθja, *substituir* sustiˈtwir or sustituˈir.

---

[1] *m* and *n* (denoting m) in the case of *b*, *n* and *l* in the case of *d*, *n* (denoting ŋ) in the case of *g*.

172. Consonant practice. The following passages should be read out for consonant practice:

(i)   ˈkarta ðe ðoŋ kiˈxote, a ðulθiˈneạ ðel toˈβoso.

soβeˈrana ˈj‿alta seˈɲora

el feˈriðo ðe ˈpunta ðe‿ɑu̯ˈsenθja, j‿el ʎaˈgaðo ðe las ˈtelas ðel koraˈθon, dulˈθisima ðulθiˈneạ ðel toˈβoso, te‿emˈbiạ la saˈluð ˈke‿el no ˈtjene. si tu βaˈlor ˈno‿es‿en mi ˈpro, si tus ðesˈðenes son‿en mj‿afiŋkaˈmjento, maˈɡwer ke josea‿asaθ ðe suˈfriðo, ˈmal poˈðre sosteˈnerme‿en‿esta ˈkui̯ta, ke‿aðeˈmas ðe ser ˈfwerte, es mwi ðuraˈðera. mi βwen‿eskuˈðero ˈsanco, te ðaˈra‿enˈtera rrelaˈθjon, o βeʎa‿iŋˈgrata, aˈmaða‿eneˈmiga ˈmiạ, del ˈmoðo ke por tu ˈkau̯sa ˈkeðo. si gusˈtares ðe‿akoˈrrerme, ˈtujo ˈsɔi̯, i si ˈno, ˈaθ lo ke te ˈbiˈnjere‿eŋ ˈgusto, ke kon‿akaˈβar mi ˈbiða, aˈbre satisˈfeco‿a tu kruelˈdað j‿a mi ðeˈseọ.

ˈtujo‿asta la ˈmwerte,

el kaβaˈʎero ðe la ˈtriste fiˈgura.

(ii)   kaβaˈʎero, saβe‿usˈte ke‿oˈra‿es?

bolˈbime, sin saˈber‿a ˈkjen se ðiriˈxia la preˈgunta, i me‿aʎe‿eŋˈfrente ðe‿uˈn‿ombre ˈno mwi ˈalto, de ˈbarβa‿i ˈpelo θeniˈθjentos, de fakˈθjones afiˈʎaðas, ke me miˈraβa kon‿unoˈs‿oxos peˈkeɲos j‿unˈdiðos‿i ðe koˈlor‿indefiˈniðo, espeˈrando, a no ðuˈðarlo, mi rresˈpwesta. komo‿el rreˈlox‿era ðe ˈnikel, eˈce mano ˈðe‿el, sin teˈmor ðe mosˈtrarlo, i le ˈðixe:

las ˈsjete‿i ˈbɛi̯nte miˈnutos.

toðaˈbia‿esperaˈremos mas ðe‿uŋ ˈkwarto ˈðe‿ora, rreˈpuso‿eˈl‿ombre rrefleˈxando ðisˈgusto‿en su fisonoˈmia.

(iii) por‿aˈʎi se ðeṣliˈθaβa la βereða, de ˈlastraṣ rreṣβalaˈðiθaṣ lo maṣ ðe‿eʎa, en θisˈθas, entre xaˈrales j‿arˈbustos‿algunaṣ ˈbeθes; ˈmucas‿al deskuˈbjerto ˈsoβre la βaˈrraŋka, eŋ ˈkujo

ˈfondo, enteneˈƀreˈθiđo por laş maˈleθaş đe‿ambas‿oˈriʎas, rrefuɱfuˈɲaƀan las‿agwaş đe lor rreˈgatoş ƀagaˈƀundos‿eŋkauˈθađas‿aˈʎi para‿ir‿a‿eŋgroˈsar por kapriˈcosoş đerroˈteros‿el kau̯ˈđal del ˈrriǫ ke se đespeˈɲaba‿a nwestra‿iθˈkjerđa j‿aˈl‿otro ˈlađo del ˈpwerto.

CHAPTER XII

STRESS AND LENGTH

173. Stress. One of the characteristics of Spanish is its well-marked stress. A syllable is said to be stressed when it is articulated with more force than the adjoining syllable or syllables. Normally, a word of two syllables or more always contains one stressed syllable. This is shown in phonetic notation by a small stroke (ˈ) preceding the initial consonant of the syllable to be stressed. In orthography, however, the stressed syllable is not always indicated; its position depends on the following simple rules.

174. (a) Words which end in a consonant (except *n* and *s*) are stressed on the final syllable, unless an accent (´) is placed over a different one, in which case that syllable is stressed. Words which are stressed on the final syllable are called *palabras agudas*.

Examples: *animal* aniˈmal, *traidor* traiˈđor, *hablad* aˈƀlađ, *querub* keˈruƀ, *carcaj* karˈkax, *reloj* rreˈlo(x), *coñac* koˈɲak, *pesadez* pesaˈđeθ, *difícil* diˈfiθil, *aljófar* alˈxofar, *áspid* ˈaspiđ, *Cádiz* ˈkađiθ.

(b) Words which end in a vowel or in *n* or *s* are stressed on the penultimate syllable, unless an accent is placed over a different one, in which case that syllable is stressed. Words which are stressed on the penultimate syllable are called *palabras llanas*.

Examples: *mano* ˈmano, *manos* ˈmanos, *lunes* ˈlunes, *cantan* ˈkantan, *cama* ˈkama, *ventana* benˈtana, *dije* ˈdixe, *lloraran* ʎoˈraran, *palmacristi* palmaˈkristi, *tribu* ˈtriƀu, *amó* aˈmo, *compás* komˈpas, *avilés* aƀiˈles, *volcán* bolˈkan, *cámara* ˈkamara, *cantará* kantaˈra, *vaivén* baiˈƀen, *alajú* alaˈxu.

175. Words which are stressed on the antepenultimate syllable are called *palabras esdrújulas*.

Examples: *álamo, célebre, águila*.

If the stress falls farther back than the antepenultimate syllable the words are called *palabras sobresdrújulas*.

Examples: *cántamelo, apárteselo*.

176. Words have the same syllable stressed in the plural as in the singular.

Examples:

> *virgen* (sing.), *vírgenes* (plur.);
> *jamón* (sing.), *jamones* (plur.).

Exceptions:

> *carácter* (sing.), *caracteres* (plur.) (not *carácteres*);
> *régimen* (sing.), *regimenes* (plur.) (not *régimenes*).

177. The student will notice that any irregular stress is marked orthographically: there are very few exceptions to this, but see § 69 (b), exception 3.

178. It is important to stress the right syllable, as sometimes the stressed syllable is the only way of determining the meaning of a word.

Example: *célebre, celebre, celebré*.

179. Some words, which have a stressed syllable in isolation, are only half-stressed in connected speech.

Example:

> *No, señor, no está el señor Jiménez.*
> no se¹por, no‿es¹ta‿el sepor xi¹meneθ.

In this example, the second syllable of *señor* is stressed in the first case, but only half-stressed when it precedes *Jiménez*. In quick conversation, the second *señor* would not be stressed at all. In a phonetic transcription of Spanish, it is not necessary to mark half-stresses.

180. Emphatic stress is used when a syllable is stressed with more emphasis than usual, as for exclamations, contrasts, etc. Emphatic stress is shown by two small strokes (ǁ) before the syllable to be stressed.

Examples:

> *¡Viva Segismundo, viva!* ǁbiƀa sexis¹mundo, ǁbiƀa.
> *¡Socorro!* soǁkorroː.
> *Digo que no.* ¹digo ke ǁno.

181. LENGTH. There are no long vowels in normal Spanish pronunciation, and there are no vowels as short as the English unstressed vowels. Length means duration of articulation and a long vowel is therefore one which is prolonged or held on longer than usual.

182. Since all the Spanish vowels are approximately of the same length, in normal pronunciation, the task of the student is not to learn when to use long vowels but to remember not to use them. Also he must remember not to obscure unstressed vowels to the neutral vowel-sound ə, as in the last syllable of *mother.*

Examples (length is shown by : placed after the sound to be lengthened):

mano	ˈmano	not ˈmaːno,
lobo	ˈloƀo	not ˈloːƀo,
cantó	kanˈto	not kanˈtoː,
no	no	not noː,
páramo	ˈparamo	not ˈparəmo,
mantilla	manˈtiʎa	not manˈtiʎə.

183. There are no long vowels in normal pronunciation, but vowels are frequently lengthened in emphatic speech, in slow speech, in dialects and in singing.

Examples: *si* siː, *pues* pweːs, *¡agua!* ˈaɡwaː (see § 41).

184. When a consonant is doubled orthographically (except *l*), it is pronounced long. This is usually shown by transcribing both consonants, but in another method of transcription only one consonant is transcribed, followed by the length sign.

Examples:

innato inˈnato or iˈnːato,
innegable inneˈɡaƀle or inːeˈɡaƀle,
sinnúmero sinˈnumero or siˈnːumero,
obviar oƀˈƀjar or oˈƀːjar,
subvenir subƀeˈnir or suƀːeˈnir.

185. When a final consonant is followed by an initial consonant of the same nature, they are pronounced as though they occurred in the same word, and are both transcribed.

Examples: *las señoras* las seˈɲoras, *un nombre* un ˈnombre, *diez zorros* djeθ ˈθorros.

186. rr, which may anyway be considered as a long r, is longer than usual when it represents *sr*.

Example: *dos rápidos* dor ˈrrapiđos (see § 141).

CHAPTER XIII

INTONATION

187. Intonation is the rise and fall in pitch of the voice when speaking. Speech may be considered, like a song, to be made up of words and music; the articulation of the various speech-sounds provides the words, and the music is provided by the intonation.

188. Just as a song will be spoilt if the singer does not sing the tune correctly (even though the words are right), so does a sentence become distorted in sound, and sometimes in meaning as well, if the correct intonation is not used. The different meanings which may be attached to the phrase *I know him* are due solely to the emotion or sentiment expressed by the intonation; the words do not change.

189. The general features of intonation are more or less the same in all European languages. Thus, it is usual to raise the voice at the end of a question requiring the answer "yes" or "no", and to lower the voice at the conclusion of a statement. But the essential difference lies in the behaviour of the voice before it reaches the ultimate rise or fall. In this respect, not only do countries differ, but regions, towns and even individuals have their own particular intonation.

190. Despite all these varieties, however, there are certain "laws" of intonation to which speakers of the same nationality all conform, and it is necessary for the foreigner to copy these if he aims at losing his foreign accent.

191. For the purpose of giving an approximate representation of Spanish intonation, the following method may be used.

Two parallel horizontal lines show the highest limit and the lowest limit of the pitch of the voice. Beneath the lower line is given the sentence or phrase corresponding to a series of dots in between the lines, which show its intonation. Each dot represents a syllable and is placed above the vowel-sound of the syllable; when there are two vowel-sounds in the same syllable (as in *teatro*) the dot is between the two vowel-sounds. Stressed syllables are shown by larger dots.

Example:

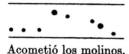

Acometió los molinos.

192. STATEMENTS. In isolated words, phrases and simple sentences, the intonation reaches its highest point on the stressed syllable of the most important word, and does not reach that height again, although it may rise a little. Sometimes, when a *palabra llana* or a *palabra esdrújula* marks the highest point of intonation in a sentence, the remaining syllable or syllables of the word maintain the same pitch as the stressed syllable.

Examples. Words and phrases of not more than a few syllables:

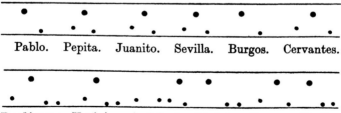

Pablo. Pepita. Juanito. Sevilla. Burgos. Cervantes.

Desdémona. Verónica. Andalucía. Córdoba. La casa. Límite·

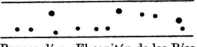

Buenos días. El capitán de los Ríos.

Short sentences:

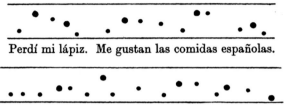

Perdí mi lápiz. Me gustan las comidas españolas.

Lope de Vega nació en mil quinientos sesenta y dos.

193. When a stressed syllable, which would normally mark the highest point of the intonation, comes at the end of a sentence, the pitch of the voice changes very quickly from a high to a low tone. The following examples show how this is represented on an intonation graph:

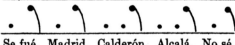

Se fué. Madrid. Calderón. Alcalá. No sé.

194. This sudden change of pitch also has the effect of giving emphasis to a statement.

Examples:

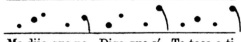

Me dijo que no. Digo que sí. Te toca a ti.

195. Longer statements, including a subordinate clause or qualifying phrase, may be divided into two "tone groups", the first of which has a rising intonation, and the second a falling one, to indicate the end of the sentence.

Examples:

(1) Antes de llegar a los postres, sonó el timbre de la puerta.

(2) En cuanto al resultado, queda en manos del Destino.

(3) El mar se ha retirado a larga distancia, y está más

tranquilo.

(4) Hablaba muy poco, aun con mi madre.

(5) No quiero pintar la grita y la zalagarda que en aquella

bendita casa se armó.

(6) Gran persona debió de ser el primero que llamó pecado

mortal a la pereza.

196. A sentence which consists of a statement qualified by various phrases or clauses is treated in the same way as the preceding examples, the sentence always ending with a falling intonation. A falling intonation may also be used half-way through an exceptionally long sentence, to avoid monotony.

Examples:

(1) Los mayóres prodigios, si son fáciles y a todo querer, se

envilecen.

(2) Si él hace el día, ella la noche: si el sol cumple los años,

ella los meses.

(3) Lisonjeado de su belleza, no me hartaba de olerlas

descogiendo sus hojas y haciendo prolija anatomía de su

artificiosa composición.

197. ENUMERATION. When words or phrases are being
enumerated, each has a falling intonation, except the penultimate one, which has a rising intonation.

Examples:

(1) He visitado a mis primos María, Angustias, Paco y

Miguel.

(2) En el invierno arraigan las plantas, en la primavera

florecen, en el estío fructifican y en el otoño se sazonan y se logran

(3) Pasma el extraordinario derroche de ingenio, la estructura

forzadamente sutil de la frase, la seca concisión y el continuo

repiqueteo de la agudeza.

198. PARENTHESIS. A phrase in parenthesis is pronounced with a low tone in intonation.

Examples:

Tienes buen gusto, dijo su amigo.

Ya se ha marchado, contestó el chico sonriendo.

199. QUESTIONS. Questions introduced by an interrogative word of one syllable begin on a high tone and have a steadily falling intonation.

Examples:

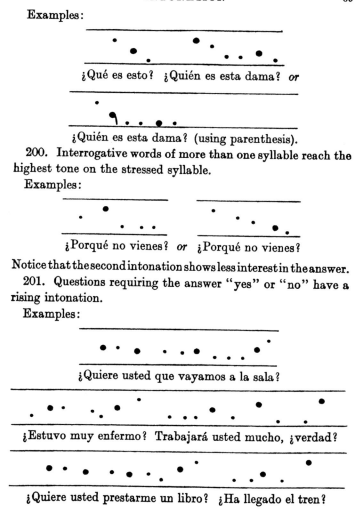

¿Qué es esto? ¿Quién es esta dama? *or*

¿Quién es esta dama? (using parenthesis).

200. Interrogative words of more than one syllable reach the highest tone on the stressed syllable.

Examples:

¿Porqué no vienes? *or* ¿Porqué no vienes?

Notice that the second intonation shows less interest in the answer.

201. Questions requiring the answer "yes" or "no" have a rising intonation.

Examples:

¿Quiere usted que vayamos a la sala?

¿Estuvo muy enfermo? Trabajará usted mucho, ¿verdad?

¿Quiere usted prestarme un libro? ¿Ha llegado el tren?

202. Exclamations and commands. These are distinguished by greater contrasts in tone, owing to the emotions they express.
Examples:

¡Oigame! ¡Ten cuidado! ¡Vaya con Dios!

¡Estupendo! ¡Qué cosa más rara! ¡Socorro!

¡Santiago, y cierra España!

203. Example of the intonation of a connected text:

Pasaron de largo por la rotonda de entrada y enfilaron el

pasillo central hasta la sala de Velázquez, en la cual penetraron.

Antes que nada fueron a la saleta de las Meninas. A Rosina

lo primero que hubo de sorprenderle en el cuadro fué la acabada simulación de ambiente y cómo los seres, a pesar de yacer

aplastadas en un lienzo, se presentaban aparentemente sólidos,

sumergidos en un caudal de aire y con distancias entre sí que

a ojo pudieran calcularse con ligero error. — ¡Qué cosa! ... —

murmuró Rosina, y se acercó al cuadro —. Nadie diría que

este caballete está pintado. Si es de bulto ... — Y se volvió

hacia Teófilo, que sonreía con afectada desdén —. Pero ¿de

veras no lo encuentra usted maravilloso? Verá usted qué

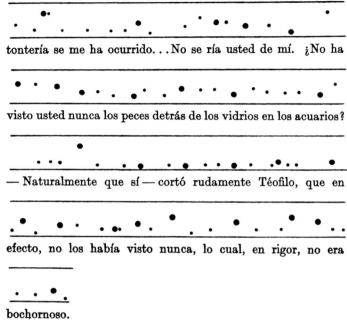

tontería se me ha ocurrido...No se ría usted de mí. ¿No ha

visto usted nunca los peces detrás de los vidrios en los acuarios?

— Naturalmente que sí — cortó rudamente Téofilo, que en

efecto, no los había visto nunca, lo cual, en rigor, no era

bochornoso.

RAMÓN PÉREZ DE AYALA.

CHAPTER XIV

PHONETIC TEXTS

204. The following passages should be read aloud. In each case, the pronunciation has been suited to the style of the piece. All the passages are in narrow transcription, with the exception of the last one.

A. Slow, careful reading.

Las sillerías de caoba con embustidos de limoncillo y asientos de tejido de cerda; el reló de sobremesa, los candelabros de plata, los espejos de vara y media altos con marco de pasta dorada; el retrato de cuerpo entero, obra del pincel de Salva o de Bardelo; el papel aterciopelado en las paredes, las cortinillas de tafetán encarnado en las vidrieras de las alcobas, y la alfombrita delante de cada puerta y de cada mueble importante de la sala, quedábanse para un puñadito de familias, cuyas mujeres torcían el gesto cuando se rozaban con el vulgo de los mortales, y cuyos muchachos gastaban las únicas levitas forradas de seda que se vieron entre sus coetáneos; no bebían agua en las fuentes públicas aunque se murieran de sed, jugando *finamente* al marro con sus *congéneres*, y antes se hubieran dejado desollar que descalzarse en la Maruca para navegar un poco en sus flotantes perchas....

PEREDA.

Narrow transcription of A.

las siʎeˈriaʂ ɗe ˈkaǫʋa kɔn‿embusˈtiɗoʂ ɗe limɔnˈθiʎo j‿aˈsjentoʂ ɗe teˈxiɗo ɗe ˈθɛrɗa; ɛl rrɛˈlo ɗe soˈʋreˈmesa, los kandeˈlaʋroʂ ɗe ˈplata, los‿esˈpɛxoʂ ɗe ˈʋara‿i meɗja ˈaltos kɔn marko ɗe ˈpasta ɗoˈraɗa; ɛl rrɛˈtrato ɗe ˈkwɛrpo‿enˈtero, ˈoʋra ɗɛl pinˈθɛl de ˈsalʋa o ɗe ˈʋarˈɗelo; ɛl paˈpɛl‿atɛrθjope-ˈlaɗo‿en las paˈreɗes, las kɔrtiˈniʎaʂ ɗe tafeˈtan‿eŋkarˈnaɗo‿en laʂ ˈʋiɗriˈeraʂ ɗe las‿alˈkoʋas, i la‿alfɔmˈbrita ɗeˈlante ɗe kaɗa ˈpwɛrta‿i ɗe kaɗa ˈmweʋle‿impɔrˈtante ɗe la ˈsala, keˈɗaʋanse para‿um puŋaˈɗito ɗe faˈmiljas; ˈkujaʂ muˈxeres tɔrˈθian‿ɛl ˈxesto ˈkwando se rrɔˈθaʋaŋ kɔn‿ɛl ˈʋuɫgo ɗe loʂ mɔrtales, i ˈkujoʂ muˈcacoʂ gasˈtaʋan las‿unikaʂ leˈʋitas fɔˈrraɗaʂ ɗe ˈseɗa ke se ˈʋjerɔn‿entre sus koeˈtaneos; ˈno ʋeˈʋian‿agwa‿en las ˈfwentes ˈpuᵬlikas‿auŋke se muˈrjeran de seᴛ, xuˈgando finaˈmente‿al ˈmarro kɔn sus kɔŋˈxeneres, i‿antes se‿uˈᵬjeran deˈxaᵭo ᵭesoˈʎar ke ᵭeskalˈθarse‿en la maˈruka para naᵬeˈgar‿um ˈpoko‿en sus floˈtantes ˈpɛrcas....

peˈreᵭa.

B. Quick dialogue.

F. ¡Dios mío de mi alma! ¿Qué es esto?...No puedo sostenerme... ¡Desdichada!

R. Señorita, yo vengo muerta.

F. ¡Ay, que es cierto!... ¿Tú lo sabes también?

R. Deje usted, que todavía no creo lo que he visto...Aquí no hay nadie...ni maletas, ni ropas, ni...Pero ¿cómo podía engañarme? Si yo misma los he visto salir.

F. ¿Y eran ellos?

R. Sí, señora. Los dos.

F. ¿Pero se han ido fuera de la ciudad?

R. Si no los he perdido de vista hasta que salieron por la Puerta de Mártires...Como está un paso de aquí....

F. ¿Y ese es el camino de Aragón?

R. Ese es.

F. ¡Indigno!... ¡Hombre indigno!

R. ¡Señorita!

F. ¿En qué te ha ofendido esta infeliz?

R. Yo estoy temblando toda...Pero...Si es incomprensible....Si no alcanzo a discurrir qué motivos ha podido haber para esta novedad.

F. ¿Pues no le quise más que a mi vida? ¿No me ha visto loca de amor?

R. No sé qué decir al considerar una acción tan infame.

F. ¿Qué has de decir? Que no me ha querido nunca ni es

hombre de bien... ¿Y vino para esto? ¿Para engañarme, para abandonarme así?

R. Pensar que su venida fué con otro designio no me parece natural...Celos... ¿Por qué ha de tener celos? Y aun eso mismo debiera enamorarle más...El no es cobarde, y no hay que decir que habrá tenido miedo de su competidor.

F. Te cansas en vano...Dí que es un pérfido, dí que es un monstruo de crueldad, y todo lo has dicho.

R. Vamos de aquí, que puede venir alguien y....

F. Sí, vámonos...Vamos a llorar... ¡Y en qué situación me deja!...Pero ¿ves qué malvado?

R. Sí, señora, ya lo conozco.

F. ¡Que bien supo fingir!... ¿Y con quién? Conmigo... ¿Pues yo merecí ser engañada tan alevosamente?... ¿Mereció mi cariño este galardón?... ¡Dios de mi vida! ¿Cuál es mi delito, cuál es?

LEANDRO MORATÍN.

Narrow transcription of B.

f. djoş ¹mio ꝺe ¹mj‿alma! ke‿e¹s‿esto?...no ¹pweꝺo soste-¹nɛrme... deşꝺi¹caꝺa!

r. seɲo¹rita, jo ꝟeŋgo ¹mwɛrta.

f. ¹aç:, ke‿es ¹θjɛrto!...¹tu lo ¹saꝟes tam¹bjen?

r. ¹dɛxe‿us¹teꝺ, ke toꝺa¹ꝟia no ¹kreo lo ke‿e¹ ꝟisto...a¹ki no‿ai ¹naꝺje...ni ma¹letaş, ni ¹rrɔpaş, ni...pero ¹komo poꝺia‿eŋga¹ɲarme? si jo ¹mişma los‿e ¹ꝟisto sa¹lir.

f. ¹j‿era¹n‿eʎos?

r. si se¹ɲora. loş ¹ꝺos.

f. pero se‿a¹n‿iꝺo ¹fwera ꝺe la θju¹ꝺaꝺ?

r. si ¹no los‿e pɛr¹ꝺiꝺo ꝺe ¹ꝟista‿asta ke sa¹ljerom pɔr la ¹pwɛrta ꝺe ¹martires...komo‿es¹ta‿um ¹paso ꝺe‿a¹ki....

f. ˈj‿ese‿es‿ɛl kaˈmino đe‿araˈgɔn?

r. ˈese‿es.

f. inˈˈdigno...ˈɔmbre‿inˈˈdigno.

r. seɲoˈrita.

f. eŋ ke te‿a ofenˈdiđo‿esta‿iɱfeˈliθ?

r. ɟo‿esˈtɔi̯ temˈblando ˈtođa...pero:...sj‿es‿iŋkɔmprensiƀle...si no‿alˈkanθo‿a điskuˈrrir ˈke moˈtiƀos‿a pođiđo‿aˈƀɛr para‿esta noƀeˈđađ.

f. pwes̬ ˈno le kise ˈmas ke‿a mi ˈƀiđa? no me‿a ˈƀisto ˈloka de‿aˈmɔr?

r. no se ˈke đeˈθir‿al kɔnsiđeˈrar‿una‿akˈθjɔn tan‿iɱˈfame.

f. ˈke‿as̬ đe đeˈθir? ke ˈno me‿a keˈriđo ˈnuŋka nj‿eˈs‿ɔmbre đe ˈƀjen...i ˈƀino paˈra‿esto? para‿eŋgaˈɲarme, para aƀandonarme‿aˈsi?

r. penˈsar ke su ƀeˈniđa fwe kɔˈn‿otro đeˈsignjo ˈno me paˈreθe natuˈral...ˈθelos...pɔr ˈke‿a đe teˈnɛr ˈθelos? ˈj‿ɑu̯n‿eso ˈmis̬mo đeˈƀjera‿enamoˈrarle ˈmas...ˈɛl no‿es koˈƀarđe, i ˈno ai̯ ke đeˈθir ke‿aˈƀra teˈniđo ˈmjeđo đe su kɔmpetiˈđɔr.

f. te ˈkansas‿em ˈbano...ˈdi ke‿es‿um ˈpɛrfiđo, ˈdi ke‿es‿um ˈmɔnstrwo đe krwɛlˈdađ, i ˈtođo lo‿as̬ ˈđico.

r. ˈbamos̬ đe‿aˈki, ke ˈpweđe ƀeniˈr‿algjen‿i....

f. ˈsi, ˈbamonos...ˈbamos‿a ʎoˈrar...j‿eŋ ˈke sitwaˈθjɔm me ˈđɛxa...pero ˈƀes ke malˈƀađo?

r. si seˈɲora, ɟa lo koˈnɔθko.

f. ke ˈƀjen supo fiŋˈxir...i kɔŋ ˈkjen? kɔˈmigo...pwes̬ ɟo mereˈθi sɛr‿eŋgaˈɲađa ˈtan‿aleƀosaˈmente?...mereˈθjo mi kariˈɲo‿este galarˈđɔn? ˈdjos̬ đe mi ˈƀiđa. ˈkwal‿es̬ mi đeˈlito, kwaˈl‿es?

ˈle̯andro moraˈtin.

C. Poetry.

(i) Ingrata beldad mía,
llegó el feliz, llegó el dichoso día,
línea de mi esperanza,
término de mi amor y tu mudanza,
pues hoy será el postrero
en que triunfar de tu desdén espero.
Este monte elevado
en sí mismo al alcázar estrellado,
y aquesta cueva oscura,
de dos vivos funesta sepultura,
escuela ruda han sido
donde la docta mágica he aprendido,
en que tanto me muestro,
que puedo dar lección a mi maestro.
Y viendo ya que hoy una vuelta entera
cumple el sol de una esfera en otra esfera,
a examinar de mis prisiones salgo
con la luz lo que puedo y lo que valgo.
Hermosos cielos puros,
atended a mis mágicos conjuros;
blandos aires veloces,
parad al sabio estruendo de mis voces;
gran peñasco violento,
estremécete al ruido de mi acento;
duros troncos vestidos,
asombráos al horror de mis gemidos;
floridas plantas bellas,
al eco os asustad de mis querellas;
dulces sonoras aves,
la acción temed de mis prodigios graves;

bárbaras, crueles fieras,
mirad las señas de mi afán primeras,
porque ciegos, turbados,
suspendidos, confusos, asustados,
cielos, aires, peñascos, troncos, plantas,
fieras y aves, estéis de ciencias tantas;
que no ha de ser en vano
el estudio infernal de Cipriano.

                Calderón, *El Mágico Prodigioso.*

Narrow transcription of C (i).

iŋˈgrata bɛlˈdað ˈmia,
ʎego‿ɛl feˈliθ, ʎeˈgo‿ɛl diˈcoso ˈðia,
ˈlinẹạ ðe ˈmj‿espeˈranθa,
ˈtɛrmino ðe mj‿aˈmɔr‿i tu muˈðanθa,
pweˈs‿ọị seˈra‿ɛl posˈtrero
eŋ ˈke trjuɱˈfar ðe tu ðeşˈðen‿esˈpero.
ˈeste ˈmɔnte‿eleˈƀaðo
en si ˈmişmo‿al‿alˈkaθar‿estreˈʎaðo,
j‿aˈkesta ˈkweƀa‿osˈkura,
de ðoş ˈƀiƀos fuˈnesta sepulˈtura,
esˈkwela ˈrruða‿an ˈsiðo
ˈdɔnde la ˈðɔkta ˈmɑxika‿e‿aprenˈdiðo,
eŋ ˈke ˈtanto me ˈmwestro,
ke pweðo ˈðar lɛkˈθjɔn‿a mi maˈestro.
i ˈƀjendo ˈʝa ˈke‿ọị una ˈƀwelta‿enˈtera
ˈkumple‿ɛl ˈsɔl de‿una‿esˈfera‿en‿otra‿esˈfera,
a‿ɛksamiˈnar ðe mis prịˈsjones ˈsalgo
kɔn la ˈluθ lo ke ˈpweðo‿i lo ke ˈƀalgo.
ɛrˈmosos ˈθjelos ˈpuros,
atenˈdeð‿a miş ˈmɑxikos kɔŋˈxuros;

ˈblandos‿aịreş ꞎeˈloθes,
paˈraꞎ‿al ˈsaꞎjo‿esˈtrwendo ꞎe miş ˈꞎoθes;
gram peˈɲasko ꞎjoˈlento,
estreˈmeθete‿al ˈrrwiꞎo ꞎe mj‿aˈθento;
ˈduros ˈtrɔŋkoş ꞎesˈtiꞎos,
asɔmˈbrɑɡş‿al‿ɔˈrrɔr ꞎe mis xeˈmiꞎos;
floˈriꞎas ˈplantaş ˈꞎeʎas,
aˈl‿eko‿os‿asusˈtaꞎ ꞎe mis keˈreʎas;
ˈduꞎθes soˈnoras‿aꞎes,
la‿akˈθjɔn teˈmeꞎ ꞎe mis proˈꞎixjoş ˈgraꞎes;
ˈbarꞎaras, ˈkrweles ˈfjeras,
miˈraꞎ las ˈseɲaş ꞎe mj‿aˈfam priˈmeras,
ˈpɔrke ˈθjegos, turˈꞎaꞎos,
suspenˈdiꞎos, kɔɱˈfusos‿asusˈtaꞎos,
ˈθjelos‿aịres, peˈɲaskos, ˈtrɔŋkos, ˈplantas,
ˈfjeras ˈj‿aꞎes‿esˈtɛịş ꞎe ˈθjenθjas ˈtantas;
ke ˈno‿a ꞎe ˈsɛr‿em ˈbano
ɛl‿esˈtuꞎjo‿iɱfɛrˈnal de θipriˈano.

kaldeˈrɔn, ɛl ˈmɑxiko proꞎiˈxjoso.

(ii)   *Arias Tristes* (Pirineos)

En la quietud de estos valles
llenos de dulce añoranza,
tiemblan, bajo el cielo azul,
las esquilas de las vacas;
se duerme el sol en la yerba,
y, en la ribera dorada,
sueñan los árboles verdes,
al ir lloroso del agua.

El pastor descansa, mudo,
sobre su larga cayada,

mirando al sol de la tarde
de primavera, y las mansas
vacas van, de prado a prado,
subiendo hacia la montaña,
al son lejano y dormido
de sus esquilas con lágrimas.
　　…Pastor, toca un aire viejo
y quejumbroso, en tu flauta;
llora en estos grandes valles
de languidez y nostaljia;
llora la yerba del suelo,
llora el diamante del agua,
llora el ensueño del sol
y los ocasos del alma.
　　Que todo, pastor, se inunde
con el llanto de tu flauta:
al otro lado del monte,
están los campos de España.
　　　　　　JUAN RAMÓN JIMÉNEZ.

Narrow transcription of C (ii).

ˈarjas ˈtristes (piriˈneǫs)

ˈen la kjeˈtuđ đe‿estoş ˈƀaʎes
ˈʎenoş đe ˈđuɫθe‿aɲoˈranθa,
ˈtjemblam, ˈbɑxo‿ɛl ˈθjelo‿aˈθuɫ,
las‿esˈkilaş ˈđe laş ˈƀakas;
se ˈđwɛrme‿ɛl ˈsɔl‿en la ˈjɛrƀa,
ˈj‿en la rriˈƀera đorađa,
ˈsweɲan loˈs‿arƀoleş ˈƀɛrđes,
aˈl‿ir ʎoˈroso đɛˈl‿agwa.

ɛl pasˈtɔr ˈđesˈkansa, ˈmuđo,
ˈsoɓre su ˈlarga kaˈjađa,
miˈrando‿al ˈsɔl de la ˈtarđe
đe primaˈɓera‿i laş ˈmansaş
ˈɓakaş ˈɓan, de ˈprađo‿a ˈprađo,
suˈɓjenˈdo‿aθja la mɔnˈtaɲa,
al ˈsɔn lɛˈxano‿i đɔrˈmiđo
ˈde sus‿esˈkilas kɔn ˈlagrimas.

...pasˈtɔr, toka‿uˈn‿ai̯re ˈbjɛxo
i kɛxumˈbroso‿en tu ˈflau̯ta;
ˈʎora‿eˈn‿estoş ˈgrandeş ˈɓaʎeş
ˈde laŋgiˈđeθ‿i nosˈtalxja;
ˈʎora la ˈjɛrɓa đɛl ˈswelo,
ˈʎora‿ɛl djaˈmante đɛˈl‿agwa,
ˈʎora‿ɛl‿enˈsweɲo đɛl ˈsɔl
ˈi los‿oˈkasoş đɛˈl‿alma.

ke ˈtođo, pasˈtɔr, se‿iˈnunde
kɔn‿ɛl ˈʎanto ˈđe tu ˈflau̯ta;
aˈl‿otro ˈlađo đɛl ˈmɔnte,
esˈtan los ˈkampoş đe‿esˈpaɲa.

ˈxwan rraˈmɔŋ xiˈmeneθ.

(iii)   *Primavera*

Era un día fresco,
un día de primavera....

Lágrimas lloraba el río,
yo sólo mis penas lloraba:
mi novia tejía guirlandas,
en la selva las aves cantaban.

Le dije — Yo voy a besarte,
porque eres mi novia amada. —
Callada, miraba el río,
y el río lloraba, lloraba.

Besé sus pétalos de rosa,
su frente serena, su cara:
entonces busqué sus ojos,
y en ellos hallé su alma....

Era un día fresco,
un día de primavera.

Narrow transcription of C (iii).

prima'ꞗera

'era‿un 'dia 'fresko,
un 'dia ꝺe 'prima'ꞗera....
'lagrimaş ʎo'raꞌꞗa‿ɛl 'rrio,
jo 'solo mis 'penaş ʎo'raꞗa;
mi 'noꞗja tɛ'xią̣ gir'landas,
en la 'sɛlꞗa la'ş‿aꞗes kan'taꞗan.

le 'Ɪꝺixe — jo 'ꞗoị̣ a ꞗe'sarte,
pɔr'ke‿ereş mi 'noꞗja‿a'maꝺa. —
ka'ʎaꝺa, mi'raꞗa‿ɛl 'rrio,
j‿ɛl 'rriǫ ʎo'raꞗa, ʎo'raꞗa.

be'se sus 'petaloş ꝺe 'rrɔsa,
su 'frente se'rena, su 'kara;
en'tɔnθeş ꞗus'ke su'ş‿ɔxos,
j‿e'n‿eʎos‿a'ʎe su 'alma....

'era‿un 'dia 'fresko,
un 'dia ꝺe 'prima'ꞗera.

D. Passage for broad transcription.

El rey Don Pedro, desamparado de los que le podían ayudar, y sospechoso de los demás, lo que sólo le restaba, se resolvió de aventurarse, encomendarse a sus manos y ponerlo todo en el trance y riesgo de una batalla; sabía muy bien que los reinos se sustentan y conservan más con la fama y reputación que con las fuerzas y armas. Teníale con gran cuidado el peligro de la real ciudad de Toledo; estaba aquejado y pensaba cómo mejor podría conservar su reputación. Esto le confirmaba más en su propósito de ir en busca de su enemigo y dalle la batalla. Procuráronselo estorbar los de Sevilla; decíanle que se destruía y se iba derecho a despeñar, que lo mejor era tener sufrimiento, reforzar su ejército y esperar las gentes que cada día vendrían de sus amigos y de los pueblos que tenían su voz.

MARIANA.

Broad transcription of D.

el rrei̥ dom ˈpedro, desampaˈrado de ˈlos ke le poˈdian ajuˈdar, i sospeˈcoso de los deˈmas, lo ke ˈsolo le rresˈtaba, se rresolˈbjo de abentuˈrarse, enkomenˈdarse a sus ˈmanos i poˈnerlo ˈtodo en el ˈtranθe i ˈrrjesgo de una baˈtaʎa; saˈbia mwi ˈbjen ke los ˈrrɛinos se susˈtentan i konˈserban ˈmas kon la ˈfama i rreputaˈθjon ke kon las ˈfwerθas i ˈarmas. teˈniale kon gran kwiˈdado el peˈligro de la ˈrreal θjuˈdad de toˈledo; esˈtaba akeˈxado i penˈsaba ˈkomo mexor poˈdria konserˈbar su rreputaˈθjon. ˈesto le konfirˈmaba ˈmas es su proˈposito de ir em ˈbuska de su eneˈmigo i ˈdaʎe la baˈtaʎa. prokuˈraronselo estorˈbar los de seˈbiʎa; deˈθianle ke se desˈtrwia i se ˈiba deˈreco a despeˈɲar, ke lo meˈxor era teˈner sufriˈmjento, rreforˈθar su eˈxerθito i espeˈrar las ˈxentes ke kada ˈdia benˈdrian de sus aˈmigos i de los ˈpweblos ke teˈnian su ˈboθ.

maˈrjana.

INDEX

Note. Symbols are printed first and are included under the corresponding orthographical headings. Thus ƀ will be found under B, x under X, etc. θ is given under T. Orthographical letters are shown in *italics.* Numbers refer to paragraphs.

a, articulation of, 39; back, 41, 42; cardinal, 18; description of, 38; examples of, 37; exercises on, 43; unstressed, 40
ɑ, 41, 42; cardinal, 18; long (ɑ:), 41
aị, 57
aǫ, 41
aų, 41, 57
-ado, pronunciation of, 129
Affricates, use of, in English, 93
agudas, palabras, 174 (*a*)
ahí, pronunciation of, 69 (*b*)
ahora, pronunciation of, 69 (*b*)
Alveolar consonants, 77, 86, 103, 112, 120, 121, 122, 141
Arabic, glottal stop in, 7; uvular plosive in, 14
Articulation, 6; organs of, Diag. No. 1
Aspiration, 80, 81, 82
aún, pronunciation of, 69 (*b*)
auxiliar, pronunciation of, 164
auxilio, pronunciation of, 164
Ayala, Ramón Pérez de, passage by, 203
Azorín, passage by, 72 (2)

b, articulation of, 85; examples of, 83; voiceless (b̥), 90
ƀ, articulation of, 126; examples of, 125; use of, 127, 134; voiceless (ƀ̥), 128
b, pronunciation of, 85, 127, 128, 169, 171
Back a (ɑ), 41, 42
Back vowels, 21, 44
Bilabial consonants, 76, 85, 100, 126, 154
bou, note on, 59 (*b*)

c, articulation of, 93, 94; examples of, 92

ç, articulation of, 144; examples of, 143; use of, 145, 146
c, pronunciation of, 78, 138, 166
Calderón, passage by, 204, C (i)
Cardinal vowels, 18
Cavity, nasal, 13
Cervantes, passage by, 172 (i)
ch, pronunciation of, 93, 95
cinc, pronunciation of, 171
Clear *l,* 112
Close lip-rounding, 47, 53, 54
Close vowel, 21
Closed syllable, 60
cohete, pronunciation of, 69 (*b*)
Commands, intonation of, 202
Consonant practice, 172
Consonants, 17; alveolar, 77, 86, 103, 112, 120, 121, 122, 141; bilabial, 76, 85, 100, 126, 154; dental, 77, 86, 103, 113, 129; double, 184, 185; flapped, 122; fricative, 124, 150, 158; interdental, 103, 113, 138; labiodental, 100, 126, 136; lateral, 114, 118; nasal, 98, 110; palatal, 107, 116, 144, 158; plosive, 7, 14, 73, 97; post-alveolar, 93; prepalatal, 93; rolled, 120; uvular, 14; velar, 88, 109, 131, 148, 154; voiced, 8, 84, 93, 98, 112, 116, 120, 126, 129, 131, 139, 142, 151, 158; voiceless, 8, 14, 75, 90, 93, 128, 136, 138, 141, 144, 148
Cords, vocal, 7

d, articulation of, 86; examples of, 83
đ, articulation of, 129; examples of, 125; loss of, 129; use of, 12) 134
d, pronunciation of, 86, 169· pronunciation of final, 130
Dark *l,* 112